journey of God's love for weak, fallen humanity. Comparing the Bible story to a true fairy tale, we're called to awaken with Christ."—*CBA Retailers + Resources*

"The greatest story ever told—that of Jesus—is retold in this book, *Story*, by one of America's most brilliant young authors, Steven James. His poetry, written in short lines with no caps, is lyrical and powerful—beautiful and often painful to read. If you want a book to make you view Jesus and the story of the Bible from a whole different vantage point, to feel his pain and the wonder of it again, this is that book to savor and treasure."—ChristianBookPreviews.com

"The greatest story ever told is recapped in short excerpts, building verse-by-verse in a modern fashion, as the reader journeys through this cleverly crafted book. From the manger to the cross, James connects the dots and uses modern-day examples to create a trendy devotional-like book that is an easy yet enjoyable read."—*CCM Magazine*

"James has a gift of relating the story of the Bible to life today. In this incredible book, professional storyteller Steven James tackles the greatest story of them all: the story of redemption. James's grasp of language is breathtaking and his power of description unequaled."—National Women's Ministries Department of the Assemblies of God

"*Story* is a book that will give you a new perspective on the intricately woven tales the Bible offers. Both deep enough for longtime believers and simple enough for the curious, Steven James has done a good job making this information interesting, humorous, understandable, and relevant."—1340mag.com

"*Story* retells the Christian story in a way that is fresh and brings new life. After hearing the Easter story in drab ways for years, it can lose its punch. Use *Story* to breathe new life into the story of Christ's death and resurrection."—Relevant Media Group

FLIRTING WITH THE
FORBIDDEN

FLIRTING WITH THE
FORBIDDEN

Finding Grace in a World of Temptation

STEVEN JAMES

Revell

a division of Baker Publishing Group
Grand Rapids, Michigan

© 2012 by Steven James

Published by Revell
a division of Baker Publishing Group
P.O. Box 6287, Grand Rapids, MI 49516-6287
www.revellbooks.com

Printed in the United States of America

Library of Congress Cataloging-in-Publication Data

James, Steven, 1969–
    Flirting with the forbidden : finding grace in a world of temptation / Steven James.
       p. cm.
    Includes bibliographical references (p.).
    ISBN 978-0-8007-3428-2 (pbk.)
    1. Temptation. 2. Bible stories. I. Title.
BT725.J36 2012
241'.3—dc23
                                      2011031814

Some of the material from "The Fine Line" is taken from *How to Smell Like God* (Standard Publishing, 2002) by Steven James.

The chapter "The Wedding" is based on material that first appeared in *Story: Recapture the Mystery* (Revell, 2006) by Steven James. Used by permission.

Some of the concepts in "Leaving the Boat" come from *Never the Same* by Steven James. Copyright © 2005 by Youth Specialties.

In keeping with biblical principles of creation stewardship, Baker Publishing Group advocates the responsible use of our natural resources. As a member of the Green Press Initiative, our company uses recycled paper when possible. The text paper of this book is composed in part of post-consumer waste.

12   13   14   15   16   17   18   7   6   5   4   3   2   1

green press
INITIATIVE

To Neil and Lisa Owen

Contents

Introduction

When my grandmother died she left me a few things. At the bottom of one of the boxes was a small photograph of a young Hispanic man. He looked maybe seventeen or eighteen years old, dark-haired, dark-eyed, and lonely. Piercingly sad eyes stared at me from the faded, scarred photograph. There was no note, no name. The upper left-hand corner of the photo was torn.

At first I was just going to throw it away, but then I studied the photo. He looked so lonely. I flipped it over once more, thinking maybe his name and identity would have magically appeared on the back. Nope. Nothing.

I asked around. None of my relatives knew who he was or why my grandmother had kept the picture.

Why is he so sad? I wondered. *What was he thinking? Who is he? And why did Grandma keep this picture and then pass it on to me?*

I ended up hanging on to that photograph. I don't know exactly why, maybe just to remind myself that he was someone's son. Someone's friend. Maybe someone's lover. And that somewhere along the line his story had intersected with my grandmother's story, and then it had entered mine.

That torn photo is the only connection I have with the story of that boy.

Most of the stuff that's really important to me is only important because of the stories that surround it—the ceramic water pitcher my great-great-aunt daintily used to pour me icy water on sweaty summer days, the rubber snake that served as the waterfront mascot when I was a counselor at a YMCA camp, the photograph of my wife and me on a nameless peak in Alaska on our honeymoon. These things only become valuable because I know the stories.

When I was growing up I would hear the tales of great heroes of faith from the Bible such as David and Moses, Samson and Mary and Saint Paul. They were "bigger than life" people. It wasn't that I thought of the stories as mere legends; I believed the people were real and had done astonishing things, but I couldn't really identify with them.

Sometimes the stories were told in a way that made it seem like God's heroes never really struggled with temptation as much as I do. They were like Joseph when he was propositioned by Potiphar's wife: "How could I do such a wicked thing and sin against the Lord?"

But over the years, I've finally realized that all of these people struggled just as much as we do. They wanted to be happy, just like we do. They wanted to find a way to deal with their guilt and shame, just like we do. They wanted people to like them, to accept them. They longed for those paradoxical human desires—adventure and security, freedom and belonging. They wanted to hope and dream and love and find meaning in their lives that was bigger than their lives.

Just like us.

And they lived on this fractured planet of heartache and cancer, of earthquakes and war, of rape and murder and lust and greed, just like us.

The stories of their struggles, their lives, their victories and failures and lessons can help us when we see how they lived with the temptations we all face.

By taking an honest look at their (and our) fascination with the forbidden, I hope you'll grow in discernment and reliance on the Holy Spirit, and develop a deeper, more intimate walk with Christ.[1]

1

Dusk

I lost two sons today.

One to his brother, the other to himself.

And I screamed.

Screamed into the darkening day.

But Death had come and there is no turning back, no rebirthing again. This I have learned. This is the lesson of my life.

Perhaps I should have seen it coming.

Yesterday, when I was preparing the morning meal with Cain, I had the small, tender sense that things had changed.

He told me that God had spoken to him, and I felt a flare of jealousy. God had spoken to me in the garden, yes, but hadn't spoken to any of us since the rift, the great divide. Since we'd been banished from the place of harmony.

"What did God say to you?" I asked my son.

He was slow in responding. "It was a message for me." I caught the hint of a grin. "Only for me."

His words were like a slap in the face.

First he taunted me and now he was drawing satisfaction from it.

"Tell me, Son. What message did God give you?"

He eyed me. "He told me that sin is crouching at my door, that it wants to control me. But that I must master it."

I was quiet. I didn't know if this truly was the Lord speaking to him, but it was a message my son definitely needed to hear and I doubted he would have come up with those words on his own.

"Then you must master the sin, Cain," I said. "The Lord will help you."

"He told me I needed to do it." A touch of venom in his words. "He never told me he would help me."

"Do not talk that way."

"Don't speak in truth? You would have me—"

"Stop." I stemmed off the argument. "Trust that God will help you and you'll be able to resist."

Then Cain smiled. "Don't worry," he said. "I'll resist."

"Don't open the door."

"I won't open the door."

It would be easier if I didn't remember the way things were in the Garden. It's the knowing that hurts, the knowing that things were different once, that harmony was possible. I wish I didn't know that, wish I could just erase the memories once and for all, forget it and live as if this were the best of all possible worlds.

But I can't.

And that's part of the curse.

It seems like so long ago when we walked with the Creator beside us. Listened to his presence. It wasn't like a voice speaking but an understanding being shared that was beyond words. We were surrounded with the overwhelming weight of his holiness, the comfort of his acceptance, the warming presence of his unspeakable love.

The memory stings like a new breed of loneliness.

When Adam looks at me I can see it in his eyes too. A longing backward through time, before all of this. A terrifying regret that we will never feel that peace again.

I used to wonder what it would be like for my boys—growing up never knowing the way things were in the Garden, only seeing splintered, thorn-encrusted glimpses of paradise. And if I have more children—if—then I wonder if there will be an eventual forgetting of what things can be like between us and the Creator, each generation falling further from the knowledge of the Garden.

The day the rift occurred is a stain on my memory. That day when death came into the world and the hot horror of shame overtook us still haunts me.

A blade cut through my heart after it happened, especially when I looked into Adam's eyes and I saw a slow-growing darkness. I found out later what it is called.

Rage.

And when the Creator spoke to us, I explained that I'd heard the thoughts, the words of the snake—which wasn't all that unusual since both Adam and I had a sense of what the animals were saying to each other. Not in the same language we spoke but in a whisper-reflection of it.

I looked to Adam for his support, for his help, but he stepped backward. Faltered. Blamed me for everything.

And all that had been pure and right between us crumbled.

I knew I would never trust him again, not like I had, and I could see by the look on his face that he had already stopped trusting me.

So much pain.

And I thought, *If death is to come, let it come! I desire it!*

But in a wicked twist of fate, the Creator let us live.

I wish he had not.

And when my sons came, despite the pain, the terrible pain of their birth, I had a sense of hope. A daring seed of belief that life would go on, that the past could be redeemed by the birth of something new.

They looked like their father. I hadn't known it would be like that.

When I awoke this morning, a tumult of clouds was roiling on the horizon. They would do this sometimes, chase us, then descend and surround us with a gray mist.

But the breath of the clouds' damp wind hadn't found us yet. The air was staid and still and sharp with the heat of the awakening day.

At the morning meal Abel announced that he was going to make an offering to God. Adam, Cain, and I listened quietly.

"An offering," I said.

"Yes. A gift."

"What gift could you possibly give God?"

Adam eyed me, trying to let his look rebuke me, but I didn't let it.

"One of my lambs," Abel said.

"How will you give your lamb to God?" Cain asked.

"I will burn it and let the smoke rise to heaven like a fragrance."

The scent of death as a gift?

"God is a spirit, Abel," I told him. "He does not need your dead sheep."

"He gives us all we have," he replied. "Everything. But what do we give him? He gives us the sun, the air, the earth, the food we eat." He smiled in his innocent way, his naive way, and I wished I could feel that sense of trust in the Creator, that pure thanksgiving, unclouded with regrets or shame. "I want to thank him."

"Then thank him by the way you live." I was done with this conversation. "Don't thank him by killing. Death is a curse, not a gift."

He was quiet.

"Let's just eat," I said, but almost immediately Adam contravened what I'd said.

"Go on," he told Abel. "Give God your offering. Who knows, he may be honored by it and bless us."

I felt anger twist me. Had I told Abel to go to the fields and make his offering, I could only guess that Adam would have told him to stay back. That's the way it was between us.

Cain cleared his throat slightly. "I'm going to give God an offering too." He didn't keep animals but gathered from the field, and I wondered what kind of offering he would give, but before I could respond, Abel nodded to him. "Good. We'll go together."

Adam was not a man to stop people from acting. He'd said nothing to me when I took the fruit, even though he was standing right beside me. And now, as our sons left, he said nothing.

The wind picked up as the deep clouds rolled our way.

When the boys had stepped away, I said, "Adam, this is not—"

"There's nothing wrong in offering to God what we have."

"Is that what you think Cain is doing?"

My husband rose quietly and headed toward the river. I might have called for him to go fetch our sons, but I did not.

And now I wonder how things might have turned out if only I had.

When the bank of clouds arrived and our sons failed to return, Adam went to find them. But somehow I already knew. A mother knows these things. Even before he returned with the body of my younger son in his arms, a deep ache had begun to gnaw at me.

Abel hung in his arms limp and still like an animal, like one of the lambs. No breath. Adam laid him down and I collapsed beside my dead son.

Dust to dust.

Then I screamed my grief into the blackened sky.

I lost two sons today.

And now I cry out to the Lord, begging him for a new life, for a new hope, and the howl of the wind on the edge of the skies is his only reply.

Now Cain said to his brother Abel, "Let's go out to the field." And while they were in the field, Cain attacked his brother Abel and killed him.

Then the LORD said to Cain, "Where is your brother Abel?"

"I don't know," he replied. "Am I my brother's keeper?"

The LORD said, "What have you done? Listen! Your brother's blood cries out to me from the ground. Now you are under a curse and driven from the ground, which opened its mouth to receive your brother's blood from your hand." (Gen. 4:8–11)

This is where it all began.

In a garden with a choice, in a field with a body. That's the legacy of humankind—the quest to be like gods, the elevation of self over others. The firstborn human murdering the second and a shattered mother weeping in the dark.

According to the Bible, things between God and humans were not always as they are now. Now we have these cliffs of pride that humility struggles to scale, these depths of despair that drown our joy, this friction between us, within us. We have arguments and grudges, fistfights and muggings, incest and abortion. None of this was in the original plan.

In the beginning, harmony existed between us and God, between us and creation, between us and each other, and, in a very real sense, between us and ourselves.

Most people feel it inside of them, a smoldering knowledge that we are not what we were meant to be; we're nagged with a hunger for eternity. Even those who reject believing in God don't seem to be able to shake the thought that a bigger purpose must be at work, a deeper joy available somewhere.

The tempter is real.

Our choices separate us from unity with the divine.

We've been cast out of the garden of clarity, of harmony, because we have sought and picked and eaten the forbidden fruit.

Here's something I've been learning the hard way: I'm never free from temptation. It might be the temptation to slant the truth in my direction when it benefits me, or to yell at my daughter when she won't stop picking on her little sister, or to lash out in anger when the world doesn't tilt my way.

I struggle with big things and I struggle with little things—anger, materialism, impatience, frustration, disappointment, and a rather unhealthy addiction to chips and salsa. Dissatisfaction in the world. The root of the fall itself.

And I've found that no matter where I travel or what I'm doing, I'm just one thought away or one action away from stepping over the line and entering the land of the forbidden.

Every day, every hour, every minute of our lives we have the opportunity to either say "yes" to God or "yes" to ourselves. That's why Jesus emphasized something I don't hear much about at churches these days—denying yourself: "If anyone would come after me, he must deny himself and take up his cross daily and follow me" (Luke 9:23). I think he found it necessary to say that because, while most of us want to do what God wants, we also want to do what *we* want. And that's where the problems begin.

Being honest about life requires that we admit we're stuck somewhere between sinfulness and holiness, between being lost and being found, between indulging ourselves and serving our God.

After all, we're both wretched and royal, sinners and saints, part of God's divine solution and part of the overarching problem.

Paul discovered that when a person trusts in Jesus Christ, the core priorities of her life fundamentally change instantly. He wrote to his friends in Corinth about this: "He died for everyone so that those who receive his new life will no longer live for themselves. Instead, they will live for Christ, who died and was raised for them" (2 Cor. 5:15 NLT). When I read those words, honestly, I get a little uncomfortable. Jesus didn't die just so that one day I could go to heaven, he died so that I might stop living for myself now.

Welcome to a paradigm shift. When I first stumbled across that verse, it was a wake-up call for me to realize that every moment I'm faced with a choice: will I offer this moment to God or try to keep it for myself?

Over the years I've read lots of books about following Jesus. Typically, they tend to make me feel guilty because I'm either not rejoicing enough or witnessing enough or going to church enough or tithing enough or praying enough.

Or they make following Jesus sound like a piece of cake: that life will just keep getting easier and easier as I get holier and holier and put into practice the Five Time-Tested Tips and Seven Life-Changing Principles that the author has based his current book, seminar series, website, or DVD curriculum on.

But I find very few books that lay out the paradoxical truth of the matter—(1) following Jesus isn't always easy, practical, fun, or popular because temptation hounds us every step of the way, every day of our lives, (2) through it all, God's grace and forgiveness are powerfully available and instantly accessible to everyone, everywhere, all the time. We live in the middle of a deep and rich paradox. Grace and truth, pain and healing woven through our world, through time itself.

The greatest saints of the ages have discovered something most of us haven't. Not only are they familiar with their own shortcomings and sins, they're also aware of the outlandish grace of God. By being mindful of both their fallen nature and Jesus's risen love, they're able to live on the escarpment of evil without constantly toppling over the side.

When we're tempted (either by our own desires or the nudgings of the devil) I don't think the point is to make us do the unthinkable—at least not at first. The goal is to make the unthinkable more and more reasonable. And then, when it doesn't seem so bad anymore, when it seems trite and harmless, when it seems like the next logical step, to have us go ahead and take a bite out of the forbidden fruit.

Ever since the tragic choice in the Garden of Eden, temptation has been the default setting for life on this planet. But most of us don't just pluck the fruit and start eating. Instead, we first get curious about what it might taste like. We wonder about the other people who've eaten it. Did they like it? Are we missing out? Isn't it unfair that they get to try some but we don't? Why should we be the only ones left out? Huh?

God never said you couldn't pick the fruit, did he? He just said you weren't supposed to eat it, right? Well, go on. Pick it . . . Good . . . Now smell it. He never said you couldn't smell it. There's nothing wrong with smelling the fruit . . . There, now, lick it. It's not the same as eating. He was clear you weren't supposed to eat it, but he never said anything about licking it . . .

And so it goes.

Until we take a bite.

It's so much easier once the fruit is in your hand, once you've touched it with your tongue.

And until we finally admit that temptation is a reality of life and that (at least to some extent) we *want* to lick the forbidden fruit and explore what lies beyond the fence, we'll remain vulnerable to the dark thoughts that keep trying to climb into our souls and burrow deeper into our hearts.

The secret to overcoming temptation is not to try harder but to receive more of what God offers: "For the grace of God that brings salvation has appeared to all men. It teaches us to say 'No' to ungodliness and worldly passions, and to live self-controlled, upright and godly lives in this present age" (Titus 2:11–12). Even the ability to say "no" comes from the grace of God.

That's how lost we are.

That's how much we need him.

That's how gracious God is.

And that's what this book is about.

2

The Fine Line

The very first time I saw her I wanted to sleep with her.

Radiant hair. Dark, deeply set eyes. She moved with the grace of women I'd only dreamed of being with.

The attraction was mutual, but there were so many reasons not to act on what I felt.

She was rich; I was a slave.

She was an Egyptian; I was a Hebrew.

She was married to my boss.

My God would not have approved.

The reasons changed in order and magnitude in my mind depending on the day, the mood, and whether or not she was standing beside me. But it seemed like the more we spoke, the less weight each of the reasons carried.

She's a woman. You're a man.

I tried to keep the reasons straight, but when a woman looks at a man the way she looked at me, a guy's convictions erode like a riverbank in a flood.

The journey to Egypt from the land of my fathers was harsh and sad. My dreams told me one thing, my experiences another. At night when I dreamt I saw honor handed to me, but my brothers gave me only pain.

First conspiring to leave me in a deep well to die.

Then deciding to sell me as a slave and at least profit a little from my disappearance.

I'm not sure what hurt worse, realizing they were about to walk away and leave me in that well to starve to death, or realizing they were selling me into a slavery that would inevitably involve beatings so fierce I might not survive.

After my brothers sold me, the nomads led me away with my wrists and ankles shackled and I was left with my thoughts of what awaited me in Egypt. For a long time I wished my brothers had let me die.

The trip took the lives of three other men who'd also been acquired as slaves, but thankfully, God gave me strength enough to survive and I arrived shaken and exhausted but healthy enough to still do the work that was put in front of me.

In Egypt, the slave traders sold me to Potiphar, captain of Pharaoh's guard. As a professional bodyguard, he wanted slaves who were athletic, strong. At the time I wasn't sure if my strength was a gift or a burden.

He brought me to his house.

And that's when I met her.

His wife, Patena.

After introducing us he was called away by one of his men and she asked me to stay for a moment.

Luxuriant features. Stately. She eyed me. "Joseph? That is what they call you?" She spoke to me in Egyptian, and though I wasn't from this country I was able to decipher that she was asking my name.

"Joseph means 'the God who saves,'" I answered in my native tongue.

A slight glimmer of a smile. "The God who saves." Now she spoke in Hebrew, finding the proper words and accents as if she were familiar with my language; I supposed perhaps it was from conversations with the other slaves she'd had over the years. "That is your name."

"Yes."

"And which God is that?"

"Yahweh, the God of the Hebrews, the Creator of the world."

She studied me until the intensity of her gaze unsettled me, and I looked away. That seemed to please her. "You have no one here?" she asked. "In this land?"

"No one?"

"No woman? No wife?"

The question held meaning deeper than the words. "I have no wife," I said. "I am pledged to no woman." I told myself that I was just answering her question, nothing more.

"Pledged to no woman," she replied softly, repeating what I'd said, turning it into a whisper.

That was all she said to me that day.

Over the next two weeks as I scheduled the servants, managed the grounds, I couldn't stop thinking of her. The more I tried to put her out of my mind, the less I was able to. I wondered what it would be like to be with her in the pleasurable ways I'd never yet been with a woman. I couldn't quiet the thoughts of her or escape them. I wasn't sure I wanted to.

Whenever she passed me in the hall or glanced my way, my heart beat faster and became knotted and tight in my chest.

Potiphar suspected nothing of the budding affection between us.

And though I did nothing to indicate to her how I felt, in time I sensed that she began to recognize the power she had over me.

I was the one in charge of the schedules of all of the servants, and, although I knew it wasn't wise, I began to make sure that the scheduling had holes in it, small vacancies where I was alone in the house. I assured myself that I had crossed no lines, broken no customs of propriety. I was just doing my job. But she noticed and one day she came to me in one of those times when I was alone.

"Joseph," she said. "The God who saves."

"Yes?"

"Come to me."

Heart racing, questions flaring, I did.

"Closer."

She waited until I was nearly within reach of her, then said, "Save me."

Trying to keep the desire from my voice I said, "From what?"

She brushed an invisible speck of something off her arm, switched the subject. "You are happy here?"

She was closer to me than the wife of another man should be.

But I did not step away.

"I am." And then I added, "Though I miss my home."

She nodded as if she understood what it's like to be sold into slavery, to be torn from the world you know, the ones you love. I sensed no condescension, just sympathy, and it seemed that she really did genuinely care about me.

And that made the moment all the more difficult.

And then her invitation—blunt, direct words that shattered me and thrilled me, sweet and alluring: "Sleep with me." Three words and nothing more, finally speaking what she had been asking me by her silences all along.

Heart racing. Racing.

I stepped back and tried to sound resolved, but my words faltered. "Please. Don't ask me to do this. Your husband has put me in charge of all of the house, keeping nothing from me—"

"Except for me."

"Yes. And my God does not allow for such things."

"Such things?" She was smirking through the words and I thought she would go on, but she chose to let me understand her however I chose.

"Yes. I could not do such a thing, such a wicked thing, and sin against my God."

I realized it sounded like a prepared speech, and in a sense, it was. I'd been rehearsing for this moment, both knowing and dreading that it would come. Two parts of me wrestling—one part longing for a chance to hold her, to go to her bed with her, to be with her, but another part hoping I could resist if the opportunity ever arose.

She let my words settle before she spoke. "So which is it? My husband or your God that you fear dishonoring?"

The question seared me. "Please, I need to get back to work."

"Yes." Her response held no disdain, but sounded more like a promise than anything else. A way of saying, without words, *"We'll speak of this again."*

I escaped the room.

But even after I'd left, her question refused to leave me alone.

Whom do I fear more—her husband or my God?

Getting caught or dishonoring Yahweh?

I knew the right answer, of course, the one I should have leaned on for strength, but I wasn't sure that it was the answer I would've given if I'd been honest with her in that moment.

Days passed.

And, despite the encounter, the attraction between us didn't ease. Nor did I take the initiative to reschedule the other servants so that I would never be alone in the house when she was around.

And she found them, the places where opportunity could slip in.

As I was secretly hoping that she would.

As I was desperately fearing she would.

Soft glances now and then, a hand brushing across mine as she passed me in the hall. "You haven't answered my question yet," she would whisper. Sultry. Inviting. She was well versed in the art of seduction, and I had all I could do to resist. One day she said to me, "First you tell me that my husband denies giving me to you, then you say that your God does as well. But I am a woman who answers not to your God—"

"But certainly to your husband."

"I answer to myself."

Despite my prayers, I found myself clinging to my aspirations of chastity by only the merest of threads. My heart refused to stop desiring her.

"Sleep with me," she asked me again and again whenever we were alone. Each time I slipped closer toward answering yes, toward the road I would not be able to turn away from once I took the first step. Then one day, she added, "It's what we both want."

"I cannot."

That night I was in the private living quarters and she entered, stood in the doorway, obstructing my way out of the room.

"Come here, slave."

I hesitated.

"I said come here."

I crossed the room. She held out her hand. "Do not run from me any longer, Joseph. I'm asking you not just as your master's wife but as a woman."

She took me in her arms and I did not run.

She ran her fingers down my spine and I did not run.

She pulled me close.

I did not run.

Then she was grabbing my shirt to take it off.

And I knew that if I did not run then, I would not run. Not ever.

I ran.

Leaving my shirt behind.

But taking my shame with me into the hallway, and out into the night.

No one else was around when he was doing his work inside the house. She came and grabbed him by his shirt, demanding, "Sleep with me!" Joseph tore himself away, but as he did, his shirt came off. She was left holding it as he ran from the house. (Gen. 39:11–12)

Joseph's story is one of the most familiar ones in the Old Testament: his brothers sold him as a slave and he was taken to Egypt, where Potiphar, the captain of Pharaoh's guard, bought him. After the incident with Potiphar's wife (who remains unnamed in Scripture), Joseph was sent to prison. Eventually, by God's sovereign grace, he became the governor second only to Pharaoh during the years of plenty and the years of famine, and was reunited with his brothers.

When I was growing up I was taught that Joseph is a "type" of Christ, a foreshadowing of Jesus. And that's why nothing bad is mentioned about him in Scripture, that's why he's always portrayed in a positive light.

That's what I was taught.

And while it's true that Joseph was used by God as a savior to his people, it's also true that he was as flawed and as human as I am. Early in the story he comes across as vain and unbothered by the blatant favoritism of his father toward him. Then toward the end of his story he's shown to be an oppressive prime minister who taxed the country into forced servitude.

And here, I believe there is also more than meets the eye in this story of his encounter with Potiphar's wife.

The Bible mentions that Joseph was well-built and handsome. We also know that God blessed him with strong leadership qualities and wisdom. So it's no surprise that he caught the attention of the women he met—single or married.

Then when his master's wife asks him to sleep with her, we hear him say, "How could I do such a wicked thing and sin against the Lord!" and when she comes on to him again, he runs off.

And growing up, that's where I didn't connect with him, because he didn't seem real. He seemed too holy, too perfect. After all, when I'm tempted I typically don't give a speech to the one tempting me and then run away so quickly that I leave my clothes behind.

Regardless of what you may have been taught about Joseph, to climb into the truth of this story, it's important that we notice that this woman's invitation to sleep with her was not a onetime occurrence.

Genesis 39:10 says that she asked him to sleep with her day after day.

Even though he was the person in charge of everyone else's schedules, she was able to keep making passes at him, so apparently he didn't alter his schedule or that of the other servants enough to avoid situations in which he would be alone with her.

Think about it this way.

The teenage babysitter flirts with the dad of the children she's watching. She invites him to hook up with her, and somehow he just happens to end up alone in the car with her. "I'll take her home, honey," he calls to his wife.

It might happen by accident once, but week after week?

Or you have an old flame who contacts you through one of the social networking sites. You just email him a few times. That's all. It's not like you're having an affair, you're just trying to stay in touch with someone who used to be important in your life before you got married.

Then he asks you to meet, and although you say no, you just happen to end up in that chat room day after day. The conversations become more and more intimate.

It might happen once, but daily?

Every married guy knows that if your boss's wife is coming on to you day after day, you avoid being alone with her. Period. So, even giving Joseph the benefit of the doubt, at best he was incredibly naive, but I doubt that. Remember, he was a sharp guy.

And then we end up with the whole incident involving his shirt.

How did she get it off him? He was a strong, well-built guy. How close were they to disrobing each other?

Here's the scenario: the boss's wife has been coming on to a striking young man for weeks. Apparently, except for refusing her advances, he hasn't taken any other steps to discourage her. He doesn't tell her that he doesn't *want* to sleep with her, only that he's *not supposed to*. And even though he could arrange it so he's never alone with her, he daily ends up with her in situations where she can proposition him and at last ends up alone in the house, in her arms.

Of course, we don't know for certain what was going through Joseph's mind, but he was a man, and just like any guy he would certainly have been flattered by the attention, tempted by the opportunity, caught up in the moment.

I'll bet that he ran away when he did because he knew that if he stayed a little longer, just a few seconds longer, he would not have been able to say no.

I think that, just like all of us at certain times, he wanted to say yes.

When I see him in this light he becomes more real to me. More believable. I can empathize with him and finally genuinely connect with his story.

I find it reassuring that Joseph was just as human as I am. It's encouraging to know that he struggled with the same desires, temptations, doubts, and fears that all people struggle with—we want to love and be loved, we want to be accepted and desired, yet, at the same time, we also want to live up to our values and morals. And sometimes these convictions and desires come into conflict with each other.

The problem for me usually isn't that I can't tell right from wrong. The problem is that I can't seem to stop myself from doing what's wrong because sometimes I actually *want* to be deceived. Because— let's just admit it—we enjoy some of the things that displease God. We like getting our way, shooting up, spreading rumors, or quietly, secretly coveting the husband or house or abs of someone else.

> Remember that the temptations that come into your life are no different from what others experience. And God is faithful. He will keep the temptation from becoming so strong that you can't stand up against it. When you are tempted, he will show you a way out so that you will not give in to it. (1 Cor. 10:12–13)

What are the ways out? Usually they're simple things like walking away, saying no, asking for help, seeking accountability. Yet, though they're simple, when we're faced with temptation they're not easy.

In light of all that, here are a few practical applications I take away from Joseph's story.

1. Pray that God will deliver you from evil.

Jesus taught his disciples to pray that God would deliver them from the evil one (Matt. 6:13). When they fell asleep in the Garden of Gethsemane, he told them to "keep alert and pray. Otherwise temptation will overpower you. For though the spirit is willing enough, the body is weak" (Mark 14:38 NLT).

On our own we're weak. We easily get overpowered. But when we pray, we're no longer on our own. We put ourselves in touch with God's powerful Spirit.

Never underestimate the power of prayer in your struggle against temptation.

2. Remove whatever leads you into sin, or remove yourself from the situation that leads you to sin.

Everyone has different areas of weakness. So identify what usually leads you away from God and then avoid those situations, activities, or people. As Jesus put it, "If your eye—even if it is your good eye—causes you to lust, gouge it out and throw it away. . . . And if your hand—even if it is your stronger hand—causes you to sin, cut it off and throw it away" (Matt. 5:29–30 NLT).

I wonder how he might rephrase that today: "If your tongue causes you to talk about people behind their backs, grab pliers and pull it out . . . if your ear causes you to listen to gossip, lop it off . . . if your foot causes you to break the speed limit, take a hacksaw to it . . . if your fingers cause you to surf to sleazy websites, snip them off."

His point?

Take sin seriously and take whatever drastic steps are necessary to remove sin-causing things from your life.

3. Promise yourself you won't sin.

A man named Job must have struggled with lust. He made a promise to himself that he wouldn't fantasize about the girls he met. "I made a covenant with my eyes not to look with lust upon a young woman" (Job 31:1 NLT). Apparently it worked. God called him "the finest man in all the earth—a man of complete integrity" (Job 2:3 NLT).

What do you struggle with? Put a name to it, and then make yourself a promise to avoid it. Put it in writing like Job did. List the TV shows or websites or people by name. The more specific you make that covenant, the better. Then remind yourself of it and tell a friend so you have more accountability.

4. Tell yourself the truth about the sin.

When I'm being tempted, I rarely tell myself the truth, either about the temptation or about the consequences of giving in to it. Instead, I just tell myself it's no big deal, that everyone else is doing it, that I won't get caught, that I won't end up hurting anyone, or that God will just forgive me afterward anyway, so what's the big deal?

Sin promises to taste delicious, but after you take a bite you discover that the aftertaste is sour. You end up with regrets and shame and confusion and hurt, only to listen to that sweet, promising voice again: "Pick me up. I'm harmless." Any time a sin seems safe, watch out.

When Jesus was tempted in the desert (see Matt. 4:1–11), he battled temptation by quoting Scripture. He used truth to conquer the subtle lies of the devil. When you're tempted, do the same. Turn to Scripture. God's Word will give you the answers, truth, and ammunition to withstand temptation—if you're willing to apply it in your life.

5. When all else fails, run away.

Just like in Joseph's life, there comes a time to run away, before you go too far.

If other people could look into our hearts, if they had the same soul-seeing eyes that God has, they'd know the truth—we're struggling just as much as they are, just as much as everyone is. But as Paul encouraged us all to do, "Let us cleanse ourselves from everything that can defile our body or spirit. And let us work toward complete purity because we fear God" (2 Cor. 7:1 NLT).

Resist when you can, flee when you have to, and seek God through it all.

Rather than seeing how close you can get to the edge of temptation, see how close you can get to the will of God.

And walk there with the strength he gives you and by the Spirit who is more powerful than your weaknesses.

3

Silence

Here's the answer he gave me: silence.

People are quick to remind me that the Lord cares, that the Lord gives us the desires of our hearts. Well, he gave me the desire for children, and now he sits in heaven, silent, watching me cry. Listening to me begging him for an answer, for a child.

I tell myself I must cling to my faith, but the years pass and my womb remains barren and my life remains empty. So what purpose does faith serve anymore?

Why would he give me this deep yearning if he only intended to use it to torture me?

What kind of a god would do that?

I've learned to stop sharing my thoughts with my husband. He tells me I shouldn't say such things about the Lord, the God of the Heavenly Armies, so I don't. But how can I help it if I think them?

And so, I've learned to keep my desperation inside where it grows ripe and hangs heavy in my heart.

If I had been Elkanah's only wife, it might not have been so bad; the shame of my barrenness might not have been so bitter. But his other wife, a sharp-tongued woman named Peninnah, does have children, and every time I see them the ache inside of me for a child of my own grows more stark. Had she not shamed me with her sly smiles and frequent reminders that only one of us was bearing children for our husband, only then might I have been able to handle my grief and shame.

But she did not let up, and the longing in my heart grew worse.

At first I had hoped that I would eventually have a child and the stinging words of my rival would cease.

But that was not to be the case.

The years passed and my prayers weren't answered.

Love is visible in the face of a man, but even more so in his actions, and I knew Elkanah's love for me was rich and real, but over time his gestures of kindness only served to remind me of how I had failed him as a wife.

Every year he would take us to Shiloh to worship the Lord and to offer him sacrifices according to our law. Elkanah would give meat to Peninnah and to her young daughters and her two sons, but he would generously give me a double share.

He felt sorry for me in his love for me; he honored me but God ignored me. I began to think Elkanah was kinder to me than God was.

Those thoughts drew me into anger, and I found that it works for a while but then it turns cold, and I clung to only a thread of hope that God would allow me the honor of being a mother before the time came when it would be too late and my childbearing days would come to an end.

With every passing day Peninnah's derision became more and more acute and more and more unbearable.

How could my husband not stop her? How could a man as good as he is marry a woman like that? He knew about the things she said, yes he did. He knew about my tears. But his one flaw was leaving us to work it out by ourselves.

I would leave the tent to worship the Lord, and Peninnah would smile and whisper, "Perhaps this year God will hear your prayers. As he has heard mine." And then she would add, "I wonder why he doesn't listen to you—"

"Stop, Peninnah."

"What sins you might have committed—"

"I said stop."

"To punish you in this way."

"Stop!"

But she would not.

And in time I could no longer keep my tears and desperation in. I lost my appetite and I stopped trying to act content, and of course Elkanah noticed. He tried to console me: "My dear Hannah, don't weep. Have something to eat. Let your spirit be lifted. A son, yes, that is a blessing, but what of your love for me? Can't that fill the place of at least two sons?"

Yes, love for him did fill my heart, but there was an emptiness he could never fill—the part of me that wanted to be a mother. However,

I had the feeling that hearing me say that would only hurt him so instead I pretended that his words had helped.

And I wept only in solitude from that day forward.

One year, my desire for a child finally became too much for me to bear. We were at our meal and Peninnah made a show of serving her sons, her daughters. My despair became so great that I fled the table, tears stinging my eyes.

At the temple I rushed past Eli the priest, who was seated on a chair near the doorpost, and I went up the steps and fell to my knees and prayed. I begged the Lord for a son.

All the years of longing, of entreating God and receiving no reply, made it harder than ever to believe, but I vowed to the Lord Almighty that if he would only hear my prayers, see my misery, remember me and my sorrow, and give me a son, then I would dedicate my child to the service of the Lord for his whole life. A Nazarite, dedicated to honoring God until the end of his days.

And rather than pray aloud and let others see my pain, I let my heart do the praying; my lips formed the words while my voice remained silent. When I lifted my eyes to the heavens, I noticed Eli watching me, but I didn't care who saw me, I only cared that the Lord would hear the cry of my heart.

Then, even as I prayed, Eli approached me, his face stern, and when we spoke his words were stones. "How long will you keep this up? Getting drunk and coming into the house of the Lord? Get rid of your wine and honor the Lord."

He thinks I'm drunk?

No! Why?

Just because I was praying silently?

"Oh no, it is not as you say!" I exclaimed. "I have had no wine, no drink. I was praying to the Lord. For years my heart has been cut in two, for the Lord has chosen not to give me a son. Please do not take me for a drunkard. I have only been praying out of the place of my pain."

I wanted to say more to him of the mockery of my rival, Peninnah, of the years of anguish as I longed for a son, but I would only have wept more.

I waited for his response. "Shalom," he said at last. "May God's peace be with you." And then he blessed me by affirming my prayer. "May the Lord, the God of Israel, the God of our fathers, honor you with a son. May he hear your request and not turn his back on your pain."

His words, his blessing, lifted the ache in my heart, and for the first time in years I felt hope that God might hear me. I went back to Elkanah and ignored the scorn and ridicule of his other wife.

And for the first time in years, my heart dared to believe.

Hannah was in deep anguish, crying bitterly as she prayed to the LORD. And she made this vow: "O LORD of Heaven's Armies, if you will look upon my sorrow and answer my prayer and give me a son, then I will give him back to you. He will be yours for his entire lifetime, and as a sign that he has been dedicated to the LORD, his hair will never be cut." (1 Sam. 1:10–11 NLT)

Soon after her encounter with Eli, Hannah did become pregnant and gave birth to a son, whom she named Samuel, which sounds like the Hebrew phrase "heard of God." When he grew up he became a great prophet and leader among God's people.

But before she recognized that her prayers were being heard by God, she went for years and years without her prayers being granted.

When I think of her I can only imagine how hard it must have been. How hard it would've been for her to hold on to her faith when she didn't see God answering her most heartfelt prayers year after year.

When you long to hear from God, when you cry out to him and he offers you no answer, no reassurances, no gift of encouragement, it's easy to slip into skepticism. It's easy to let either despair or doubt eat away at your faith.

It's happened to me. It's happened to most people I know. Sometimes doubt leads to anger; sometimes anger leads to doubt. But neither leads to peace.

In this book I'd like to tell you about a few of the answers to prayer I've gotten over the years, but I should tell you something first: I'm not the kind of guy who thinks God speaks to him every day or does so audibly in a movie star voice with an English accent. But I do know that there have been a handful of times when I've been praying and I've heard an answer to my prayer, or a rebuttal to my complaint, that I've known didn't come from my own heart.

Once when I was having a hard time feeling love toward someone, I said to God, "I don't love this person. When I act loving I feel like a hypocrite!" And I heard the reply, "Treating people in a loving manner is not hypocrisy, it's Christianity."

Another time I was struggling with witnessing to someone and I told God, "I'm just trying to share Christianity with him," and I heard, "Ever try living it out?"

Ouch.

That one was like a fist in the gut.

Then on a trip to Guatemala with Compassion International, I awoke early one morning and walked across the rooftop and gazed up at a volcano overlooking the city. I was praying about the difficulties of love and I distinctly heard, "It is in love that we are born."

Still, there have been many, other times when, just like Hannah, I have prayed and heard no answer.

Most people I know, whether they're Christians or not, have gone through a stage in which they ask, "Why is this happening to me? Why am I depressed, or divorced? Why am I hurting, or poor, or alone? Why did that happen to me, God?"

Why me?

It can be a question born out of intense pain, or in some cases, a question brought as a challenge to God's mercy and justice.

Even Jesus while he was suffering on the cross called out the question to the silent heavens, "Why, God! Why have you forsaken me?"

No, our prayers might not all be answered in the time and manner we'd prefer, but we can either turn our eyes inward in pity or upward in faith.

The temptation to give up on God is always real and often present, but the answer lies in persistence and trust. As Jesus said,

Ask and it will be given to you; seek and you will find; knock and the door will be opened to you. For everyone who asks receives; he who seeks finds; and to him who knocks, the door will be opened.

Which of you, if his son asks for bread, will give him a stone? Or if he asks for a fish, will give him a snake? If you, then, though you are evil, know how to give good gifts to your children, how much more will your Father in heaven give good gifts to those who ask him! (Matt. 7:7–11)

God is kinder and will always give good gifts to us, even better ones than we can dream of.

I think that to truly follow Jesus, we have to ask not just that God's will be done in this world, or in our lives, but that his will be done in our wills. His Spirit can shape and transform our wills (Rom. 12:1–2) if we will stop resisting and start submitting.

Pray that your faith, your will, your perseverance would be strengthened by his Spirit. Let hope be born anew, whether he gives you what you desire most, or what he desires more.

As he specializes in doing.

Now to him who is able to do immeasurably more than all we ask or imagine, according to his power that is at work within us, to him be glory in the church and in Christ Jesus throughout all generations, for ever and ever! Amen. (Eph. 3:20–21)

4
We Dined

My poetry has suffered.

I used to wake early here at the palace and watch the sunrise, just as I did when I was younger working as a shepherd.

Those were the times I would write my songs. Before the little pieces of the day began to fall into place, before the weight of the undone began to press heavily on me. I would write and something within the sunlight and the dawn and the stillness gave birth to the songs.

I sang to my God, my King. Unashamed—my voice carrying far across the valley.

And for a while I did the same here at the palace, sang and wrote in the mornings, but in time I began to sleep in a little later, to miss the dawn, to let the songs slip away. And so I would return to the old songs, the ones I'd written before, and I would lean on them for the reassurance that I really was a songwriter.

A subtle place inside my heart had lost its moorings. Even while it was happening I was aware of it.

The story has been told and retold now. I was in the palace. The ramparts had been built in such a way that I could see nearly all of Jerusalem, and I remember, in those days, looking across the city and thinking about all the people below me, going about their lives in safety, the safety I had helped win for them.

People went to their roofs for privacy and she was there, bathing. I didn't look away. And then, everything spun so quickly, quickly out of control. I knew I'd seen her before, but her name escaped me, so I called for one of my servants.

Found out her name was Bathsheba.

The wife of Uriah, one of our soldiers at the front.

I had my servant fetch her.

When she arrived I walked downstairs and saw her, so beautiful. A dove had landed in my home.

"You are the wife of Uriah the Hittite?"

"Yes, your majesty."

"He is a brave warrior of whom I am proud."

"Yes, your majesty."

She was stunning and young. Her eyes demure.

"And you are Bathsheba."

"Yes."

We dined.

And she spent the night.

Later, when I found out she was pregnant I tried to arrange for her husband to sleep with her so no one would know the child was mine, but he refused, saying that if the men in the field could not sleep beside their wives, neither would he.

I felt a sting of shame, but at the same time I wasn't ready to let it bud into repentance. Instead, it grew into anger.

I arranged for Uriah to be sent to the front and for the men to withdraw so that he would be killed, and when the time of mourning was over, I married Bathsheba.

Yes, the story has been told and retold now.

And whenever I hear it I can feel the fire of guilt again.

My secret was not as hidden as I'd thought.

One day, soon after my child had been born, Nathan, the one who spoke for God, came to me. "Your majesty, I have a message from the Lord."

"Tell it to me."

"There was a certain man who had much land and cattle and many flocks. Another man had only one lamb and it slept in his arms like a daughter. One day a traveler came to the rich man's house. Instead of taking one of his own sheep to feed the stranger, the rich man took the poor man's only lamb. He slaughtered it, roasted it, and fed it to the traveler. And so, your majesty, I am wondering, what should be done to that rich man?"

As someone who'd spent many years as a shepherd, I was outraged. "He is a wicked man and deserves to be killed."

Without hesitation Nathan said, "You are the man."

And everything inside of me that I'd been hiding from broke loose in a sharp crack of shame.

Sorrow chased by fear.

A poem cut through me and fell bare and raw on the page.

Have mercy on me, O God,
    according to your unfailing love;
according to your great compassion
    blot out my transgressions.
Wash away all my iniquity
    and cleanse me from my sin.
For I know my transgressions,
    and my sin is always before me.
Hide your face from my sins
    and blot out all my iniquity.
Create in me a pure heart, O God,
    and renew a steadfast spirit within me.
Do not cast me from your presence
    or take your Holy Spirit from me.
Restore to me the joy of your salvation
    and grant me a willing spirit, to sustain me.
Then I will teach transgressors your ways,
    and sinners will turn back to you.
You do not delight in sacrifice, or I would bring it;
    you do not take pleasure in burnt offerings.
The sacrifices of God are a broken spirit;
    a broken and contrite heart,
        O God, you will not despise.[2]

I came to a place where I had to admit, confess, repent, or fall headlong into the trap I'd laid for myself.

And I made my choice.

Then David said to Nathan, "I have sinned against the LORD."
Nathan replied, "The LORD has taken away your sin." (2 Sam. 12:13)

My favorite book title of all time is *Yes, Lord, I Have Sinned, But I Have Several Excellent Excuses* by James W. Moore. I wish I would have thought of that title because I could have definitely written a book like it.

I can almost always give you a reason for my failures, a complete and unabridged explanation with footnotes and a detailed bibliography and plenty of appendices of supporting facts and figures to explain why I committed that trespass.

And unless I get caught, I almost never change.

Once when I was younger I was at a Barnes and Noble bookstore and I found a full-color, illustrated book in the art section filled with paintings of sexy women in sleazy, skintight lingerie. Most of the models were posing like cats.

It's not pornography, I told myself. *It's art.*

I was about halfway through the "art book" when I heard someone call my name. "Hey, Steve."

I looked up, my heart racing. One of the pastors from my church was walking my way. He was less than ten feet away.

Oh no!

"Whatcha reading?" he said.

I fumbled to stick the book back on the shelf, but he saw it. He refrained from commenting, but his look said it all.

Over the years, I've gotten caught with my hand in the cookie jar more often than I'd care to admit.

It's fascinating to me, and a little disheartening, that no one really learns the lessons that matter most the easy way.

We only learn the hard way.

That's how stubborn and blind we are.

Imagine that you have a swimming pool full of alligators and you're so devious and heartless that you're trying to convince someone to jump into the water. How would you do it?

I can think of at least four ways.

1. Convince the person that alligators aren't dangerous.
2. Blindfold him before letting him near the pool.
3. Add something to the water that makes it murky and hides the alligators.
4. Lure the person close to the edge so he can see the gators for himself, and then when his back is turned, push him in.

It's probably unnecessary to walk you through the spiritual application here, but I will say that it's a lot more common for me to jump into the water on my own than to be pushed in.

Too many times when we share the gospel we neglect to mention that every moment from his conversion on, the new convert will be engaged in a wrestling match with himself, that as soon as he conquers one pet sin, another will squirm free and start coming at him all over again. Paul wrote in Romans 7, "I do not understand what I do. For what I want to do I do not do, but what I hate I do. . . . I have the desire to do what is good, but I cannot carry it out. For what I do is not the good I want to do; no, the evil I do not want to do—this I keep on doing. . . . I want to do good, evil is right there with me."

So, what do we do with guilt?

Some of the most common ways are deception (convincing ourselves the wrong isn't really so wrong), reversal (convincing ourselves the wrong was really right), and diversion (distracting ourselves from honestly addressing the wrong).

All of these are ways of trying to minimize accountability. We rationalize, we justify, we tell ourselves it was no big deal, that we're not as bad as the other guy, or we come up with excuses that we would never accept from anyone else but that we expect God will accept from us.

Yes, Lord, I've sinned, but I have several excellent excuses.

Paul's solution? He concluded in Romans 7:24–25, "Who will rescue me from this body of death? Thanks be to God—through Jesus Christ our Lord!"

Who is a God like you, who pardons sin and forgives the transgression of the remnant of his inheritance? You do not stay angry forever but delight to show mercy. (Micah 7:18)

Don't miss out on the power of confession.

Wallowing in guilt is a subtle form of pride because the focus is on you, not on God. It's on your failures, not on his goodness. Your attention isn't drawn to grace, but to shame, and your eyes are on overcoming your past rather than promoting his kingdom.

One time when I was doing that, God spoke to me and said, "Whenever you're focusing on your disappointments rather than my grace you're worshiping something other than me."

How does it benefit the kingdom of Christ to have its fallen warriors, its wounded and hurting saints, continue slashing themselves with their enemy's words? Don't replay your pain. Allow God to do what he does best, heal hurting souls.

It takes faith and humility to accept God's forgiveness, but when you understand that no matter how far you fall, God's grace goes deeper, and no matter what you've done, God's love is greater, it sets you free in all the ways that matter most.

Just as it did for David, a man who ended up being known as a man after God's own heart (Acts 13:22). Because "if we confess our sins, [Jesus] is faithful and just and will forgive us our sins and purify us from all unrighteousness" (1 John 1:9).

Yes, Lord, I've sinned, but you've forgiven me forever.

That's more like the book I'd like to live.

BEYOND THE MIRAGE
BEYOND THE MIRAGE
BEYOND THE MIRAGE
BEYOND THE MIRAGE
BEYOND THE MIRAGE
BEYOND THE MIRAGE
BEYOND THE MIRAGE
BEYOND THE MIRAGE
BEYOND THE MIRAGE
BEYOND THE MIRAGE
BEYOND THE MIRAGE
BEYOND THE MIRAGE

5

Beyond the Mirage

I go for walks in the early morning while the dew is still heavy on the ground. Some days the mist rolls in from the lake, gently curling tendrils that climb into the day, lingering as long as possible before the sun wisps them away.

All so temporary.

Pebbles crunch underfoot now as I return to the palace and watch the day awakening all around me.

Soon I will hear the news.

As soon as I get back to the palace.

But now, I smell lamb roasting, see women heading to market. I pause to watch the smoke rise and then disappear as smiths fan their hearth fires into flame. Children are already in the streets chasing each other and laughing.

They laugh because they don't realize what awaits them.

I've dressed in common clothes today, and since people see what they expect to see, they don't notice that it is their king walking among them. After all, rulers live in palaces. The richer that people get, the farther they move away from the poor. Yet still, the underprivileged in the villages envy the rich, but to what end? They hope to have their wealth without their worries, but the two are as inseparable as a mother bear and her cub.

The morning walk has brought me no relief from my burdened thoughts, though, only added to the heavy spirit within me.

The palace is just ahead. The guards at the gate know me in this guise, but they are the only ones. They'll let me through, and only when I change clothes will the people recognize me, honor me again.

A set of clothes is ruling them.

"Your majesty." The guard, a man named Ari, lowers his head in reverence.

I rest a hand on his shoulder. "How is your wife? Your son?"

"Very well, O King."

"And the soldiers, have they returned?"

A pause. "No. And I have heard no word concerning their mission."

"Thank you." Disappointed, but I try not to show it. "Shalom."

"Shalom."

I enter, and the vacant halls echo my footsteps.

I don't want this anymore. Any of this. The affairs of state, the privileges that they bring. After forty years of ruling I feel less qualified than ever to make the decisions that shape a nation.

Yes, of course, there are pleasures to be had, so many wives and concubines to comfort and divert me from the questions, but pleasure is as impermanent as the morning mists. You might try to capture it in your hand, but just when you think you've grasped hold, it slips through your fingers and is gone.

I pass through the halls shimmering with the gold that I've brought from lands far across the sea. Walls of the finest cedar from Lebanon. But why? One day this palace will pass from me to my oldest son, who did nothing to earn it—and what is the meaning in that? Even the smiths in town will work their whole lives and for what? A small pile of possessions, a humble home that will be given to another when they die. Meaningless.

Mist.

I decide to wait for the soldiers in the library.

I enter and survey the thousands of scrolls in their carefully constructed slots in the walls. Descriptions of birds and reptiles and all manner of fish and animals. I've read them all and I remember so much, too much.

Because facts fill nothing inside of me that really needs to be filled.

I've heard whispers in the halls of the palace and I know that others envy this gift I have, this gift of memory, but they don't see the dark side of it. There's a curse embedded in all knowledge, because the clearer you understand the world, the more meaninglessness you will see. All the animals, all the plants die just as we do, and who's to say we're any better off than they are? We live, we suffer or thrive, we die, and I wonder if it wouldn't be better to be a stillborn child, passing into the grave without having to see the meaninglessness, without having to experience the grief and heartache and pain of the waking world.

Taking one of the scrolls, I read for a while, not to learn, just to distract myself. But in the back of my mind the thoughts of futility refuse to leave me alone.

Most people live their lives buried deep in the trivial urgencies of life, because stepping back and looking at the mists of all you accomplish, of all your wisdom and dreams evaporating around you, is too painful, too terrifying. It's much easier to either close your eyes or fill them with so much activity that you have no time to rest and think and reflect.

I set the scroll aside.

The soldiers will be here any minute with word about Jeroboam—if he was caught, if he was killed. One life in lieu of many.

But still, I know his death would be on my hands.

I wait.

Death.

And life.

Since this world is passing away, lasting hope could not possibly come from within it. For how could something eternal be found in the temporal? What hope does death offer? What hope does the grave hold? Hope must be a gift from another place or it would ultimately be no hope at all.

Here's what I know: life is a mystery. Death is a certainty. Hope, if there is any to be found, is a gift.

I've worshiped the gods of many lands and found only hollow relief, and I'm left thinking that meaning is only a mirage in the desert. We spend our lives scrambling across the sand, trying to get closer to it, but even as we approach, it eludes us, disappearing and leaving us parched and alone in the dry heat of the day.

My thoughts are interrupted by the sound of a soldier walking through the hall.

So.

Now.

The news.

But a moment later the sound of his footsteps fades. Then disappears.

So it is not the men bringing the news.

And I am left in silence again.

What is taking them so long?

At the window I gaze across the city.

All the mists are gone now.

The temple of the Lord, the only God who has ever spoken to me, the God of my fathers, stands to the left. My father planned the project and I spent years constructing it. Now it shines in the early morning sun.

They arrive.

Two soldiers, and they bow before me.

"Rise," I say. They stand and their faces tell me the news even before they can speak it. "Is he alive? Did he escape?"

They know that their lives lie in the balance. If the young man was able to get away I will certainly take their lives—at least that is what they think. But today I've decided I do not want their blood spilled. But I don't tell them this because I want them to think they'll die.

"He has escaped, your majesty," one of the young men whispers. "To Egypt. King Shishak has welcomed him." I see fear and finality in his eyes.

He waits.

I do not speak.

So, now Jeroboam, a man I'd put in charge of rebuilding and refurbishing the walls around the city, has turned against me and has become my enemy. My rival to the throne.

Or, when I go the way of my fathers, at least the rival to the reign of my son.

Mist.

I let the soldiers stand there thinking of death, reeling in the anticipation of it, until finally I dismiss them and they leave with a sweep of relief. An awareness of the moment.

They step away more alive than they came, having looked so closely into the eyes of death. A gift wrapped in a cloth of fear.

Life isn't fair—the wicked prosper, the righteous are oppressed; the wise are forgotten, fools are honored. The fastest runner sometimes loses the race; the strongest warrior is sometimes defeated. A kingdom is given to a foreman rather than a king's son. Fate and chance and destiny rule, and however much we may complain we will never overcome the inequalities of life.

Though I am in the palace, I feel as if I'm standing in the desert feeling the tepid wind in my face, seeing the shimmers of heat-born waves against the ground.

This is the way of our world. The way of all ambition and success—they're all mirages with promises this life can't fulfill; luring me further from the very things I need the most.

What lies beyond the mirage? More desert, or a place of refreshment and celebration?

That is the question that haunts me daily.

Sometimes it seems like the desert is all there is.

Sometimes it seems that hope lies beyond the horizon.

And the best way I can put my conclusion: I hope that there is hope.

But I'm not sure any longer.

"Meaningless! Meaningless!"
　　says the Teacher.
"Utterly meaningless!
　　Everything is meaningless."
What does man gain from all his labor
　　at which he toils under the sun?
　　　　　　　—Solomon, as he reflects on the seeming futility of life
　　　　　　　　　　　　　　　　　　　(Eccles. 1:2–3)

If I were an atheist, there's one book of the Bible that I'd be able to agree with 99 percent of—Ecclesiastes.

Ecclesiastes is starkly honest about the harsh realities, the unfathomable inconsistencies, the brutal injustices of life. Solomon makes many modern-day believers uncomfortable since he offers more questions than answers. His book rolls forward like an elaborate, irrefutable argument from a philosophical atheist.

And when you read the book's pages you can't help but notice that Solomon's observations are true. He gives example after example of the injustices of our world. They resonate in you and you know that even though his conclusions might not be a prism reflecting every angle of truth, they are at least a window peering unflinching at certain aspects of the truth of our world.

The inequalities.

The injustices.

The apparent meaninglessness . . .

But.

More on this in a minute.

First, a bit of background.

Solomon followed David as Israel's king. Early in his reign, when God asked him what he desired most, he asked for wisdom and discernment—not just great knowledge, but the ability to put it into practice in order to be a ruler who could faithfully reign and justly judge what was best for God's people.

Because he chose this, God gave him even more than he asked for—unparalleled riches, long life, and peace in his kingdom.

But with his wisdom came the double-edged blade of deep questions and an unquenchable curiosity about the meaning of life. He searched for answers and meaning in pleasure and sex, in entertainment and work, in accomplishments and knowledge, in wealth and indulgence, in wine and foolish behavior; he even admits that he denied himself nothing that his heart desired (Eccles. 2:10).

But he discovered that, in the big scheme of things, all of these diversions were ultimately meaningless since death and inequality affect us all:

1. Despite our best-laid plans and intentions, nothing is certain in life except for death (Eccles. 7:14; 9:12).

2. Life isn't fair or just or kind, so we shouldn't be surprised by injustice, suffering, or pain (Eccles. 8:14).

This quest for meaning is one of the deepest and most persistent theological and philosophical questions humans have ever had. After all, if we all die in the end despite how much we might accomplish or dream or sacrifice, what's the point of it all? Is there any ultimate purpose to life?

At the heart of all these questions lies a deep temptation, one of the most disheartening and devastating ones of all—hopelessness.

And so, what do we typically do to avoid it?

Well, we usually frantically distract ourselves so we don't have to think about it. We fill our lives with urgent and trivial diversions to make sure we're never still enough to have to look our mortality in the eye.

As philosopher and author Peter Kreeft put it, "We want to complexify our lives. We don't have to, we want to. We want to be harried and hassled and busy. Unconsciously, we want the very thing we complain about. For if we had leisure, we would look at ourselves and listen to our hearts and see the great gaping hole in our hearts and be terrified, because that hole is so big that nothing but God can fill it. We think we want peace and silence and freedom and leisure, but deep down we know that this would be unendurable to us."[3]

So in essence, we avoid thinking about death.

But conversely, Solomon suggests we do the opposite.

> It is better to go to a house of mourning
>   than to go to a house of feasting,
> for death is the destiny of every man;
>   the living should take this to heart.

Sorrow is better than laughter,
  because a sad face is good for the heart.
The heart of the wise is in the house of mourning,
  but the heart of fools is in the house of pleasure. (Eccles. 7:2–4)

We live in a counterfeit world where image is everything, appearance is more important than substance, and reputation trumps integrity. Life becomes a show. Ambition, when it's not wedded to God's will, always results in disrupting, rather than advancing, his kingdom.

It's sobering to realize how much of our lives we spend in the futile and time-consuming task of becoming and looking more successful than the very people Jesus has called us to serve and honor above ourselves. Solomon noticed this absurdity thousands of years ago.

Then I observed that most people are motivated to success because they envy their neighbors. But this, too, is meaningless—like chasing the wind. (Eccles. 4:4 NLT)

We decorate ourselves with makeup and muscles and jewelry and hip clothes and designer cell phones and $60,000 cars and homes that are finely tuned to match the image we're so carefully constructing for people we don't even know.

There's nothing sadder than someone who has spent his whole life pursuing things that are worthless to God.

Solomon's conclusion?

A God-centered life is the only one with ultimate purpose and lasting meaning. With God we live in the paradox of meaninglessness and meaning. Every moment becomes imbued with purpose amidst the suffering and grief of living on a heartbroken planet.

Hidden within Solomon's quest is an acknowledgment of the futility of finding ultimate purpose in anything other than God.

Our world is a prelude to eternity. We hear faint echoes of the coming themes, drawing us forward into the music of the eternal, but the echoes never quite fulfill the longings they ignite. Usually, happiness dances just out of reach, just over the next horizon, just beyond the next purchase. In those rare instances where we actually do find joy, it doesn't last. Thrills are short-lived. Even love fades away, but those soul longings for eternity stay put. This world is both a gift and a hint—it's a gift for today and a hint of tomorrow. And the themes won't be resolved until the final movement.

Although Solomon doesn't delve into this in the book of Ecclesiastes, the hope of eternity brings each moment new meaning, true meaning, deep and lasting meaning.

Here are a few thoughts to keep in mind when the mirage appears, when the hopelessness seems inescapable.

1. Settle into grace. God doesn't accept us because of our accomplishments; he doesn't define us by our successes. Turning to him, resting in him, pursuing your relationship with him brings purpose to the otherwise mirage-laden days.
2. Beware of anything that promises more than God does. God offers peace within the turmoil of life, not a quick deliverance from it. Anything that makes that promise doesn't come from him.
3. Enjoy the moments you've been given. Enjoy your work and your rest, your friendships and your family. These are all gifts

that God gives you, and most people pass through their days without ever opening the packages.

Sometimes I have to remind myself that every moment of my life is currency from God. How will I spend it? On my priorities or his? On my goals and agenda or his? God isn't asking me to fix the future, just to receive this present moment as if it were a gift from him, however cleverly disguised it may be as normal, everyday life.

Solomon concluded that there's no secret formula to life. As hard as we try to, we'll never figure out all its twists and turns and seeming injustices. It didn't make sense to Solomon, the world's wisest man. And it's not always going to make sense to us. But there is a trail beyond the mirage that leads to a true oasis.

One that will satisfy our hearts in the deepest, longest-lasting ways possible.

6

Famine

Bitterness is the flavor of my life.

I know how it tastes, not on my tongue, but in my heart, flowing through me, darkening all of my days.

I know what it's like to see your love turn sour. I know what it's like to watch your life turn cold.

It was a drought that sent me and my family traveling from Bethlehem to Edom, a land where food was available.

My husband and two sons were hard workers and it didn't take us long to raise enough money to buy a small home, make a new start.

Both sons found wives. At first I wasn't excited about them marrying these Edomites, but both young brides turned out to be good women and I knew they would one day be good mothers.

And whenever my husband would hug me and call me by my name, it would remind me of all that we had, all we'd been given. "Naomi," he would whisper. My name meant "beautiful," and he was fond of reminding me of that. "You have the only name that is fitting for you."

I thought joy had moved into our home. A full family. A full life. A future to look forward to.

But then, my new life began to unravel. Every thread of my contentment pulling apart.

It was the fever.

And nearly all who suffered from it succumbed.

And if only they'd died more quickly, it would have been evidence, at least small evidence, of God's grace.

But they did not.

My husband was the first in our family to die.

It took him a long time.

The day he finally passed away and I held his still body and wept, a deep fracture broke open inside me.

And then, in the midst of my grief, my two sons became ill. And even though I survived, the part of me that had looked forward to the future withered.

When I buried my first, then my second son, I also buried any hope I had of joy being reborn in my life.

I had nothing against my daughters-in-law, but I also had nothing except them to keep me here in this land. They needed to find new husbands, and they were young enough that they would not have a problem.

But me?

No.

There was nothing for me in that land. Only harsh reminders of the past—of the famine that drove us here, of the fever, of my dead family. I couldn't live in that country of jagged memories, so I decided to return to my hometown and try to start over.

Ruth begged to come along.

At first I thought it was simply duty, a kind gesture toward a middle-aged widow, but she persisted, saying that she would leave her people, leave her land, her gods, and adopt mine.

I didn't know how to tell her that the God she was promising to serve was a God I wasn't sure I wanted to believe in anymore. He'd abandoned me here. I searched for a way to explain, but I saw the loss and loneliness in her eyes and said nothing.

She's a widow just like you. Don't forget that. And she still believes that life can be different, that life can be better.

I didn't have the heart to shatter that illusion. And so I agreed, and we made the long journey to the town that used to be my home.

Bethlehem.

The day we arrived was filled with sun and dust and simmering heat. As we approached the houses that lie on the outskirts of town, my throat was dry, my eyes sore from battling the sun.

My friend Bakura was the first to see me. And she called out loud enough for the other women to hear.

"Naomi!" she cried. "Naomi! Is it you? After all this time, have you come home?"

She meant her words as gifts, I knew that. But the meaning of my name turned the words into barbs. I pulled away from her embrace.

"No," I said. "Naomi is dead, buried in another land. She lies with her husband, beside her two sons. Call me Mara."

I watched Ruth as I said the words and I saw her eyes drift to the ground.

"Mara?" Bakura said. "Bitter? I will not call you 'Bitter.'"

And all the anger, all the loss, all the sorrow rose inside me and found its way into my voice. "Yes," I said. "That is my new name."

"But—"

"I went away full and I came back empty." My words were ripe with anger. "And it is God Almighty who has brought this bitterness into my life. Call me Mara. That is my new name. Beauty died in Edom."

At last, when she had left, I told Ruth to come with me, and I noticed that she touched away a tear. I had the sense that she wasn't just crying because of the loss of her husband but because of me.

She was so young.

So naive.

I turned away and began looking for a place for us to stay.

Thankfully, in one small touch of mercy, we arrived in Bethlehem at harvesttime.

I had just enough money to rent a room for Ruth and me to share. We'd used up all our food and water on the long trip from Edom.

"Ruth," I called, and she came immediately. "I'll get some water from the well outside of town. You go to the fields. Gather any grain that's left after the men have passed through the fields, after they've taken all that they need, gather only what is left, not what is standing."

"But is that not stealing? Is that not against the laws of your God?"

"It is not stealing." I should have perhaps told her that it was the way of our God to provide for the widows and the orphans, to teach his people to care for the poor. That would've been the right answer. The kind of answer one is taught to say, but I didn't believe those words anymore. "It is community," I said, leaving God out of my explanation.

She was the foreigner now, to a people who were not accustomed to welcoming foreigners, but I hoped the men in the field would not bother her.

"But which field?" she asked.

I thought for a moment, trying to remember the names and faces of any relatives or friends who wouldn't turn a foreigner away. At last I told her a name, she left, and I headed for the well.

I returned to the house before she did, and when she arrived, she had more grain than we could eat in a month.

The stalks! She didn't listen and took from the stalks!

Though the people in town knew me, I could only imagine the outcry when word spread that the woman staying with me, the Edomite, had indeed stolen grain.

I put my hand on her shoulder, gripping more tightly than I should have. "Where did you get all that grain?"

"The field you told me to visit." A whisper of fear crossed her face. "The owner, Boaz, he told his men to leave extra for me. I took only what they left for me. I swear by the God of Israel."

I let go of her.

Boaz was a distant relative of mine.

She was waiting for my reply. "I swear," she said.

I believed her then, but my thoughts shifted to what she'd said a moment earlier, to her mention of Boaz.

Our laws provided the legal privilege for a relative to marry widows of their relations to keep the family name alive.

He was a kind man; I knew that already, and it only took me a minute of asking around to find out he was not yet married. I could hardly believe it.

"Ruth," I said. "When you saw him, what did you think of him?"

"What did I think of him?"

"Yes." It'd been several months beyond the time of grieving for my son, her husband. "You're a woman, he's a man. What did you think of him?"

Her soft blush told me.

I walked to the corner of our room where I'd stored our clothes and the little perfume that we owned.

"What are you thinking, Naomi?"

Mara. Call me Mara!

I held out her best outfit to her. "I'm thinking that any man would be a fool not to look your way when you're wearing this."

I waited at the house for her.

I'd sent her to the field. Even the best men tend to relax with wine at harvesttime, and I had a feeling that Boaz would not be an exception. After a few too many drinks I expected he would sleep at the winepress for the evening.

"Lay at his feet," I'd told her.

"And then what?"

"When he wakes up, remind him that you're single and available. Your perfume and your clothes will give him the message."

She arrived home at dawn.

"How did it go?" I asked her.

Ruth smiled.

And I was almost tempted to as well.

Their child arrived today. A boy.

Ruth named him Obed.

Bakura was the first to whisper to me, "Naomi, God has given you a new child to help raise."

Don't call me—

I looked into Obed's eyes.

You went away full and came back empty.

But here I was holding a new kind of fullness.

When I didn't reply to her, Bakura said, "Naomi? Are you all right?"

"Yes." I did not correct her, did not ask her to call me Mara.

Not anymore.

My name is Naomi.

My name is Beautiful.

From now on.

The women said to Naomi: "Praise be to the LORD, who this day has not left you without a kinsman-redeemer. May he become famous throughout Israel! He will renew your life and sustain you in your old age. For your daughter-in-law, who loves you and who is better to you than seven sons, has given him birth."

Then Naomi took the child, laid him in her lap and cared for him. (Ruth 4:14–16)

I know how easy it is to go away somewhere full and come back empty. In my life and in the lives of the people I know I've seen people go into jobs full of ambition and come back empty, into marriages full of dreams and come back devastated, into college full of aspirations and come back with disappointment.

Our world is stained with the bitterness of the undone, the unsaid, the unfulfilled, broken dreams and promises, shattered lives and families.

Fractures that run deep, bitter, raw and real.

Everyone I know has had times when they descended from hope into despair, from beauty into bitterness.

They've traveled from being Naomi to becoming Mara.

We end up in bankruptcy, in divorce, in loneliness. And when we do, it's not hard for emptiness to turn into blame, and blame to turn into bitterness.

Look around and you won't have to look far to find reasons to be disappointed at life or bitter at God. One time when he was struggling with despair, David wrote, "Be merciful to me, LORD, for I am faint; O LORD, heal me, for my bones are in agony. My soul is in anguish. How long, O LORD, how long? Turn, O LORD, and deliver me; save me because of your unfailing love" (Ps. 6:2–4).

It's hard to see sometimes, but also vital to realize, that our world is filled with majesty, grace, compassion, and love just as much as it is filled with emptiness and loss and unthinkable violence and suffering.

Some people close one eye to the pain and pretend that life really isn't so bad. Some people close the other eye. They don't see the beauty, only the pain.

Truth has both eyes open.

And sees both the terror and the wonder.

Good fortune deceives, but bad fortune enlightens. With her display of specious riches, good fortune enslaves the minds of those who enjoy her, while bad fortune gives men release through the recognition of how fragile a thing happiness is.

—Anicius Boethius, Christian philosopher,
poet, and politician (480–524)

Over the years, just as in all marriages, my wife and I have gone through some difficult times, especially when our children were younger. For a long time both of us were lonely and felt disconnected from each other.

I remember watching my hopes of having a happy and fulfilling marriage disappear. And one day I was praying (i.e., complaining) to God and I said, "People tell me I have to sacrifice to have a happy marriage. What more do you want me to sacrifice? If she wants money, I give her money. If she wants to spend time together or talk or have me do the dishes, I will. What more do you want me to sacrifice? Do you want me to give up my happiness?"

And, I heard this answer: "Would you be willing to give up your unhappiness?"

I was stunned. I had no reply.

Disappointment had become the default setting for my life, and he was asking me to let it change to joy.

In a sense I was calling myself Mara.

He was asking if I'd be willing to be called Naomi.

To let go of bitterness and embrace the beauty of life again.

One of the best ways to shift your focus from disappointment to joy is to turn your eyes from your problems to your blessings.

Your wounds and struggles and choices and victories have helped shape you into who you are, but the past has not shaped you into who you will become. That's up to you as you cooperate with God, and that depends on the choices you make today and the perspective you have when it comes to gifts he graciously gives amidst the pain.

Remember, Naomi and Ruth arrived in Bethlehem at just the right time of year, on just the right day. Ruth ended up at just the right field and met just the right man at just the right time. God was working the background, weaving a new kind of fullness, a new kind of beauty born of pain.

At times we all question God. At times we won't see the threads of meaning behind our circumstances, but he's always there, working in the background to produce something even better than we could dream of. God is working in ways we cannot see to accomplish greater things than we could ever imagine.

Keep in mind that since disappointment is so often connected to relationships, work on loving others rather than trying to be loved by them. As pastor and teacher Eberhard Arnold wrote, "I beg you:

stop concentrating on your desire to be loved. It is the opposite of Christianity."

Honestly, I think this is part of the appeal of Facebook, Twitter, and the other social networking sites.

People will post their status on Facebook and be offended or feel slighted if no one responds to it or comments on it. As Blaise Pascal, the seventeenth-century mathematician, wrote, "We do not content ourselves with the life we have in ourselves; we desire to live an imaginary life in the minds of others, and for this purpose we endeavor to shine."

Most social networking is an attempt to live an imaginary life in the minds of others.

Vanity disguised as status posting.

And when people don't think of us as much as we want or as highly as we want, we get offended and resent it. Why? Because pride has so entangled our souls that it has convinced us that we should be more important in their minds than other people are.

Or that thoughts of us should be filling their minds rather than thoughts of God.

Which is really a form of narcissism.

I've found that serving others helps me to stop obsessing about myself and my pain and get a proper perspective on the world again.

I have to remind myself that when tragedy comes, things will never go back to normal. Circumstances will change, yes, and eventually settle into a new kind of normal, but time moves on and so does life. Scripture reminds us to set our eyes on the future, to gaze into the possibilities of eternity, rather than dwell on the failures of the past.

It's easy to play the victim in a world where pain is a given. Since we all die, grief and even bitterness are certainties. But God is always available, offering a new kind of fullness. Even when he's silent to our prayers and invisible to our eyes, he is never ambivalent about our pain.

And he specializes in turning bitterness into a new kind of hope. A new kind of beauty.

That lasts forever and is available to all who are willing to accept it.

7

The Wedding

He stood waiting, expectant, his hand outstretched. But I hesitated. After all, I'd never danced with a rabbi before. Alon, my husband of twelve hours, gave me a little nudge. "Go on, Rachel," he told me.

"Yes," I said finally. "Okay."

"Thanks," Jesus said. I took his hand and he led me onto the dance floor. Everyone nodded and stepped to the side to let the young rabbi dance with the bride.

"I love weddings," he whispered to me.

And we began to dance.

The night before, I thought I was going to go crazy. I peered out the window again and again, waiting, wondering. What could be taking so long?

I scanned the dark street. Nothing. No torches. No lanterns. Nothing. Crickets jabbered at me from somewhere in the shadows outside my window. Other than that, the night was quiet.

My father walked up behind me and put his hand on my shoulder. "He'll get here when he gets here. Stop worrying. Have something to eat."

"But what if I miss him? What if he's not coming?"

I heard my dad sigh. And within his sigh I heard something else. Music? Or maybe it was the wind—

"C'mon, have—"

"Shh, Father! Listen!"

There it was again!

I scanned the street. Yes! Yes. There. A torch! And also a sound, a song rising in the night!

"They're coming!" I cried.

"'Bout time," my father grumbled. "I was beginning to wonder."

I could barely contain myself. The music and laughter echoed through the town now. People were stepping outside their homes along the narrow street and clapping to the rhythm of the drums, holding oil lamps to light the way for the wedding procession.

Dust rose into the air, curling around the laughing torches. The whole town was dancing to my door.

Then I saw my groom.

"Rachel!" he shouted, and stretched out his arms. I burst from the house and into the music and the warm swirl of his embrace. I caught the smell of myrrh on his cheek and leaned against the strong depth of his chest.

Around us everyone, everyone, was dancing.

My mother had spent all afternoon weaving golden thread into my hair. Now, as I took Alon's hand and danced with him toward our wedding, my hair fluttered behind me as if it were alive. As soon as we arrived at his house my aunts and cousins would braid it with pearls handed down from a dozen generations. We weren't rich, but my father spent all he could to help me look like a princess. It was my night. My wedding. Everything was perfect.

When Alon and I finally arrived at his house, he paused at the door. "Rachel. Your father has said yes to our marriage, but I would rather have your approval than his. You know once you step across the threshold of my home—"

"We're married forever."

"Yes. And I don't want you to come in unless that *yes* comes from your heart and not just your father's."

In our country only a man of men would offer his bride such a choice. Without hesitation I stepped forward and through the doorway.

And that's when the real party began.

Everything was a whirlwind of sounds and lights and laughter. The giggles of little girls twirling around in their prettiest dresses. The shouts of young men trying to outdo each other on the dance floor and at the wine cup. The quiet smiles of grandparents as they watched the wedding and the reception unfold.

And my husband, Alon, that dark curl of hair falling over his left eye, the feel of his beard against my cheek when we kissed, the strength of his hands around my waist.

Every moment was a girl's dream come true.

A young rabbi had come; my parents had invited him. At one point he stood and offered a blessing to our union and a prayer for our happiness. He was dancing a lot too. He seemed to really be enjoying himself.

But a few minutes after the blessing and the toast I noticed it. Something wasn't right. Just an undercurrent of confusion at first, whispered conversations between my mother and the rabbi. More whispers. Then nods.

There's a problem, I thought. *There's a problem at my wedding.*

Weddings are a big deal where I live. The party can go on for a week or more. Usually, it's at the groom's house. So Alon's family was hosting us. Sometimes more people than you expect show up and you don't have enough food on hand. Or enough wine. And believe me, if there's one place you don't want to run out of wine it's at a Jewish wedding.

Jesus's mother was whispering to him, then a few minutes later I saw him speaking with the stewards.

I watched from a distance. The waiters were acting strange. Stealthy. They went to the water vats and the next thing I knew they were handing out wine cups all around, laughing. I edged over to the vats and looked inside them.

They were filled with wine. Hundreds of gallons of wine.

What?

I glanced at Jesus. He smiled at me, raising his cup.

Wine? But how?

I hurried over to tell Alon what was going on, but the caterer in charge of the banquet stepped between us, smiling broadly, swaying slightly. Apparently, he'd been doing his best to assure that the wine was suitable for the guests to drink.

"You," he said, winking at Alon. "You sly dog you!"

"What is it?"

"Everyone serves the best wine first—*hiccup*—and then when the guests have had a little—*hiccup*—too much to drink they pull out the cheap stuff. But not you! Oh no—*hiccup*—" He raised his cup high. "You saved the best for last!"

My husband looked curiously at the caterer and then at me. "I did?"

I nodded toward Jesus, who was finishing a dance with one of the bridesmaids. "Yes," I said. "You did."

"Ah yes," Alon said vaguely, still clueless.

The master of the banquet raised his cup again, took a long swig, and mumbled to himself, "I could use a refill, I think. Yup, saved the best for last."

He wandered off and Alon turned to me. "What's going on?"

"You're not going to believe what I just—"

But before I could say another word I felt a hand on my shoulder. I turned. Jesus.

"Congratulations, Rachel," he said, his eyes twinkling. He was a bit out of breath from the last dance.

"Thank you." I felt myself blushing not from attraction but from amazement.

"I love weddings."

"I can see."

Then, he shook Alon's hand. "Now, you take good care of this bride of yours."

Alon nodded reverently. "I will, Rabbi."

Jesus leaned close. He spoke to Alon in an urgent whisper, but I heard every word. "Treat her like a queen, my friend. Love her as Yahweh loves Israel. Love her as Yahweh loves you."

Alon paused for a moment before answering. Now it was his chance to say yes. "I will, Rabbi. Yes. A queen."

Ah, Alon. My Alon! A man of men! I held his arm with both of my hands. I never wanted to let him go.

Jesus smiled. "Good. Now, I'm sure you won't mind if I steal a dance from your bride, your queen?"

"Of course not."

Then the rabbi bowed to me and held out his hand.

Alon nudged me. "Go on, Rachel."

"Yes," I said finally. "Okay."

So I danced with Jesus as everyone else stood around singing and laughing and raising a toast to my marriage with glasses of this young rabbi's bubbly, sparkling, intoxicating miracle.

"Oh, I love weddings," he said.

"I can see," I said as he twirled me faster through the night.

This miraculous sign at Cana in Galilee was Jesus' first display of his glory. And his disciples believed in him.

—The apostle John remembering the day Jesus kicked off his preaching ministry by turning a truckload of water into vintage wine (John 2:11 NLT)

Maybe it's just a coincidence that Jesus chose to kick off his public ministry by attending a wedding, but I doubt it. The more I learn about him, the fewer coincidences I see.

Here's the context: Jesus is thirty. He has spent the last decade or so working as a carpenter and has just recently shifted careers to become a rabbi. He was baptized, went on a retreat, prayed, fasted, withstood temptations from the devil, and recruited a handful of followers. You'd expect those sorts of things from a religious leader. No surprise there. But then . . .

Does he found a church? Nope.

Apply for nonprofit status? Nope.

Go door-to-door peddling his worldview? Nope.

Instead he takes a group of his wine-guzzling drinking buddies to a weeklong wedding celebration, and when it looks like things are winding down, he turns 150 gallons of water into the best wine money can buy just to keep the party going.

That's my kind of rabbi.

Jesus loved to party and was often disparaged by the religious fundamentalists because of it. One time he told them, "No one puts new wine into old wineskins. The new wine would burst the old skins, spilling the wine and ruining the skins. New wine must be put into new wineskins" (Luke 5:37–38 NLT). When God became man he offered new wine to thirsty souls.

I'm thankful Jesus didn't come to start another religion. We have too many of those already. And I'm thankful Jesus didn't come to give us another set of laws or rules or regulations or advice. Our world has enough of those too.

Instead he came to give us a fresh spiritual connection with God. As he told his followers, "Are you tired? Worn out? Burned out on religion? Come to me. Get away with me and you'll recover your life. I'll show you how to take a real rest. Walk with me and work with me—watch how I do it. Learn the unforced rhythms of grace" (Matt. 11:28–29 Message).

Jesus came to pour new wine into our hearts and new hope into our souls.

Our lives seem so complex, yet when we finally stop striving for satisfaction, pleasure, security, relaxation, comfort, and convenience, what's left? For most of us, not much.

But Jesus offers us something different and long-lasting. Rather than the frenzied pursuit of our self-indulgence, self-realization, and self-gratification. His answer is simple—deny your self altogether. As philosopher Peter Kreeft wrote, "If there is any one message all our psychopagan prophets insist on, it is that we must love our selves. But if there is any one message that Jesus and all his saints insist on, it is that we must deny our selves."

Sometimes this means abandoning our dreams and ambitions, our goals and philosophies, our agendas and good intentions. It might cost us our treasures, our relationships, our self-esteem, our self-determination. Often it means wrapping our hearts and lives and minds and time and resources around the things that matter most to Jesus, rather than to us. Always it means weeding the things out of our lives that hold us back from total commitment.

At times I think we're all tempted to create caricatures of God that diminish him, that shrink him down to a comfortable, manageable size, but Jesus rages against our misconceptions.

Some people picture God as a harmless doddering grandpappy in heaven. But in truth, he's more like an impassioned young lover swinging his bride across the dance floor. Jesus didn't arrive on earth to debate theology but to propose marriage. In a very real spiritual sense, God is courting us.

Christianity is wild. It's intimate. It's heartbreaking and soul-mending. It's the wings to rise above the everyday and the hope of a honeymoon with the God who has loved you forever.

The party has just begun and the best is yet to come.

UNDERCURRENTS UNDERCURRENTS
UNDERCURRENTS UNDERCURRENTS
UNDERCURRENTS UNDERCURRENTS
UNDERCURRENTS
UNDERCURRENTS UNDERCURRENTS
UNDERCURRENTS UNDERCURRENTS
UNDERCURRENTS UNDERCURRENTS
UNDERCURRENTS
UNDERCURRENTS
UNDERCURRENTS
UNDERCURRENTS

8

Undercurrents

Yes, it's true what they say; Jesus and I were close, especially at the beginning. But even though I tried to do my best to bridge the gap that eventually formed between us, in the end, he had a different agenda, and as hard as it is to say, I think most of the problems that developed between us came from his side, not mine.

When he first started preaching I did what I could to help spread the word about his message, about who he was. It seemed like the least I could do, trying to help out, to get people interested.

Early in his ministry I tried to reaffirm to him how much I believed in him, how much power he could have if only he would expand his vision, but he never seemed interested in becoming all he was meant to be. And that's when I began trying to figure out how best to move him into the public spotlight.

After John the Baptist was imprisoned for speaking out against the king, a man who'd taken his brother's wife to live with him as his own, Jesus began to pick things up right where John left off, telling people that the time had come to turn from their sins, that the kingdom of God was near: "Repent and believe the good news," he would say. "For the kingdom of God is at hand." It'd been John's message, and now it was the Lord's.

Some people accepted it, but many, including me, were hoping that, rather than simply reiterating what his predecessor had said, Jesus would have something more substantial to share. I told them to be patient. To wait. To trust. And some did.

But some did not.

They left him, went their own way.

It was hard to know how best to encourage Jesus in those days when I saw people who'd once been close to him, question him and then walk away.

Now, looking back, I think it was because at the time there was a lot of confusion about the kingdom of God and what it meant and whom it actually referred to. Many Jews thought of it only in terms of a political uprising to throw off the tyranny of the Romans, but I was familiar enough with the prophecies throughout the ages to know that it meant so much more than that. God had always been more interested in transforming the inner lives of people than toppling the regimes they lived under, however oppressive they might be.

Honestly, I've always thought that anyone who read the prophecies should have realized those things, but when religion gets ahold of people, it almost always blinds them. They tend to start thinking inwardly, only about what's best for themselves and the other insiders, rather than focusing their thoughts outward, toward what's good for the community as a whole.

So when the Lord began to preach this news of repentance, of a transformed kingdom of acceptance that included social outsiders—thieves, prostitutes, homosexuals, even Gentiles—the people were troubled. The crowds who did follow Jesus were more interested in the glamorous miracles and the hope of political regime change than in any genuine change of heart.

I wasn't exactly sure what to do about all that. I understood what he was saying, or at least I thought I did, and I knew he was speaking in broader terms than just establishing another government in place of the one that was in authority. But he was the teacher. He was the one in charge. I wasn't in a position to elucidate his message to the crowds.

And then came the day in Capernaum.

It was a cloudy, damp Sabbath and Jesus went to teach in the synagogue.

A few of my friends and I went to listen to him, and even as he was speaking, I could see how amazed everyone was. People began to whisper to each other about how he spoke with authority, how he wasn't like the other religious teachers. "Who is this man?"

The murmuring stopped when a man possessed by an evil spirit stood and the man cried out, "What do you want with us, Jesus of Nazareth! Did you come to destroy us?" A chilly stillness tightened in the air. People began to edge toward the door. "I know who you are," he shouted, "the Holy One of God!"

"Quiet," Jesus roared. "Out! Come out of him!"

And then, the spirit shook the man like a rag, threw him to the ground. He shrieked with an unholy cry.

Then, only stony silence.

No one moved. It felt as if the room itself were holding its breath.

Jesus went to the man and took his hand, helped him stand. Presented him to everyone, restored, in his right mind. "He's free," Jesus said softly, and the man stared around the room with clear eyes, not wild and crazed like they'd been only moments earlier.

Everyone was stunned. Questions scampered through the crowd. "Who is he? What kind of authority is this? Even evil spirits obey him."

I eased out the back and watched Jesus walk along the road with James and John. I wanted to go to him, talk with him about what had just happened. But, unsure how he might respond, I held back.

Despite everyone's amazement and awe, truth be told, there was an undercurrent of fear in the town. Could a man this powerful be trusted?

I heard that he healed Pete's mother-in-law of a fever that night. I wanted to spread the news about what he'd done—first freeing the man from the evil spirit, then healing a woman who'd been critically ill—but I didn't need to. By sunset, it seemed as if the whole town was gathered outside his door.

He had compassion on people. He healed the sick and he cast out more demons, as the crowd all watched in amazement.

I left just before dawn. But I couldn't stay away. When I returned at first light the crowd had gathered again—some people might've even been there all night. But Jesus wasn't there. I wondered if all of this publicity he was receiving so early in his ministry career was getting to him. If it was going to help him long-term or not.

Pete told the crowd, "He went to pray. We'll find him. Just wait here. Don't worry."

Then he and Andrew and John went to look for Jesus. I tagged along at a distance. I wasn't part of the inner circle. As far as I could tell they didn't even know I was there.

Andrew pointed toward a hill. "There he is, Pete. Let's go."

The Lord was sitting by himself looking across the lake. The early morning sun lay low in the pregnant sky. The mood of the day remained uncertain.

Pete ran to Jesus and asked what he was doing. "Everyone is looking for you." I heard a knot of excitement in his voice, but also a gentle rebuke. I sensed that Pete was thrilled to be on the wave of something big. A tide turning his land and his people toward freedom.

I wasn't certain, but I guessed that since his mother-in-law was the first one healed the day before he had a personal stake in things. However, I could tell it was more than that. As excited as he was about the healing, I had the sense that he also anxiously wanted Jesus to establish this kingdom, the one he'd been preaching about.

Jesus remained quiet as Pete encouraged him to return. "The crowd, the people, they're waiting for you. You have to—"

"I have to?" he replied. "I have to what?"

"Heal them." But despite Pete's typical brash confidence, these words sounded more like a question than an answer.

"No. I came to preach. The villages nearby haven't heard. I need to tell them about the kingdom. That's why I'm here. That's why I've come."

I watched carefully and I couldn't be sure, but I thought I saw disappointment in both Pete's and Andrew's eyes.

"To preach," Pete said. "Yes. Okay. To preach."

The people of Capernaum weren't happy to see the Lord leave, but he didn't seem to care. Managing his public image wasn't turning out to be his specialty.

Jesus began to travel, just as he'd said he would, going all over Galilee, teaching in the synagogues and driving out evil spirits.

And despite his reticence to enter the public spotlight, word spread throughout the region. More crowds gathered.

In those days as I followed him, I'd hang back on the outskirts of the crowd, taking it all in. Sometimes I'd venture ahead to the nearby towns and tell people that he was coming, whisper to people about his power. And then, they would be waiting for him with their sick, with their demon-possessed, with their infirm when he arrived.

One day I met a man with leprosy who'd heard about Jesus. I urged him to see the Lord himself. As Jesus and his retinue approached the man's village, he ran up to Jesus and fell on his knees, begging to be healed: "Please. You have the power; I know you do. If you only say the word. If you are willing, please . . ." He bent low and pressed his forehead to the dirt. A small crowd was hurrying out to see what would happen. "Heal me," he begged.

Despite what the people around him would undoubtedly say, Jesus touched the man.

You do not touch a leper. Not ever. People gasped. Some backed away. Others began to murmur that he was not a prophet, could not possibly be a prophet if he was willing to touch an unclean man.

But Jesus just stood there with a gentle hand on the man's shoulder. "I am willing," he said. "Be clean. Be healed. Be free."

Jesus helped him to his feet, and to everyone's astonishment, the leprosy was gone. Jesus hadn't just stopped the disease; he had reversed it. The fingers that the man had lost were restored. He was whole again. He would never be excluded from the temple, or shunned, or mocked. Not only was his disease gone, but the stigma of his disease as well.

Truly, it was astonishing.

Jesus saw the crowd forming and pulled the man aside. I was close enough to hear his words. "Do not tell a soul what happened."

The man was staring at his hands. The people were hurrying toward Jesus.

The Lord took the man's chin gently but firmly in his hand, directed his eyes toward his own. "Listen to me. Go to the priest; offer the sacrifices commanded by Moses. You are clean, you are whole, but honor the law in this way so that all propriety is carried out. Do you understand?"

"Yes." But the man was distracted, eyes on the crowd, perhaps planning to shout the news to them before going anywhere.

"Tell me again," Jesus urged. "Say it."

Finally, the man looked at Jesus and sounded earnest. "Yes, Prophet. I will not tell."

He was too stunned by what had happened to even thank Jesus.

But when the man left he did tell. He did spread the word.

I was pleased. It meant things were changing.

And as a result, Jesus couldn't travel openly anymore. He had to move around at night, and when he arrived in a town, no one seemed all that interested in his message about the kingdom of God, instead they wanted healings, miracles, signs of his power.

So, for a while he tried to stay outside of the towns, to teach small groups his message, but the crowds followed him.

And, maybe I should be ashamed, but I admit it—I was encouraging people to spread the word just like the leper had done. A man with Jesus's potential was not a man who should be hiding in the shadows, isolating himself. He was the most powerful man I'd ever met, and keeping his presence a secret didn't seem to serve the greater good.

Better to keep him in the public eye. Make sure everything stayed out in the open.

His miracles went on, and he began to sharpen his message, announcing not only the coming of the kingdom of God but claiming to have the power to forgive sins—not just the sins that others committed against him but the sins that people committed against others.

Obviously, this created quite a stir among the religious leaders. "Blasphemy," they exclaimed. "Only God can forgive sins!"

And they were right. Jesus's claims were staggering and a little unsettling.

But he backed up his words with his amazing authority over disease and disability and evil spirits. It's easy to say that you can forgive sins, so he chose to do what's more difficult in order to prove that he could do what was easy. After all, wasn't it at least possible that a man who could heal bodies could also restore souls?

However, the upper echelon of the religious community felt threatened by his words and his miracles, and understandably so. They weren't just shocked that he would make such outrageous claims, they were troubled by what he was able to do.

So despite his popularity, a stain began to spread across his reputation. And when he started going to parties with people who were known to be swindlers, when he began to show disdain for the sacredness of the Sabbath, when he began to compare the religion of his friends and family to cracked and dried wineskins that were about to burst under the weight of his new teachings, things only got worse.

The conflicts sharpened, and then one Sabbath day it all came to a head.

As was his habit, he was teaching in the synagogue, and some of the religious leaders were there—not just to hear him as he poured out some of this "new wine teaching" that he claimed to have, but also to try and find something in his message that contradicted the laws of Moses.

And the wineskins burst open.

A man whose hand had become shriveled by some kind of disease was there and Jesus invited him to stand up in front of everyone, then he said to the teachers in the crowd, "The Sabbath, this holy day that is so special to you. You make laws to protect it, but it was never meant to be protected. It's there to serve you, not be served by you. What is the Sabbath for? Evil thoughts? Evil plans? Or the healing of souls crushed by the pain of this world?"

No one spoke.

He went on, his words becoming more and more pointed. "Is this a day to give birth to what is new or to cling to what is old? To take lives or to save them?"

Still, no reply. But you could feel the air in the room grow taut.

Then, he told the man with the withered hand to uncurl it, to straighten it out. And for a moment I wondered if Jesus was mocking him.

But as the man obeyed, his hand opened like a flower. He held it high.

Completely healed.

That was the day. Rather than rejoice with the crowd, the leaders took offense at Jesus's tone and teaching. They began to plot how to kill the Son of God.

And I smiled.

My plan had worked.

Spreading the words, accusing him of the very thing he claimed to be, and keeping him in the public light, I had turned the tables on him for good.

I might not have been able to tempt Jesus to sin in the wilderness all those months ago, but I had helped cause his death and the end of this kingdom he was so fond of.

Yes.

They don't call me Satan, the accuser, for nothing.

Our struggle is not against flesh and blood, but against . . . the powers of this dark world and against the spiritual forces of evil in the heavenly realms. (Eph. 6:12)

One day as I was reading the first three chapters of the book of Mark, it struck me that there were two stories being told simultaneously, the story of Jesus as he spread light, and a parallel story of the forces of darkness rallying against him.

Move.

Countermove.

The more he healed, and the more demons he drove out, the more his popularity rocketed and the less people were interested in his message. They wanted miracles from him; he wanted repentance from them. It was as if the forces of darkness were using Jesus's compassion against him.

However, God's plan was so big that he was able to take the death of his only Son and turn it into the salvation of humankind. Despite all the apparent victories of Satan (infiltrating Jesus's inner circle, eventually possessing Judas, turning the religious leaders against Christ, orchestrating the betrayal in the Garden, overseeing the torture and death of Jesus), God came out ahead. And what looked like the ultimate defeat was really the final and certain victory for all who believe.

Jesus never joked around about temptation. Three of the Gospel writers mention the famous account of his temptation in the desert (Matt. 4:1–11; Mark 1:12; Luke 4:13). At the time, the devil appealed to his physical needs (turn these rocks into bread), his faith (jump off this building, let's see if God saves you), and the very real human tendency toward ambition (bow and worship me and I'll give you all this land, as far as you can see).

I find great comfort in the fact that Jesus was tempted in every way I am, yet remained sinless (Heb. 4:15). He understands what it's like to be on the brink of coveting, lusting, worshiping wealth, letting ambition lead you around by the nose.

It's not a cliché to say that we gain spiritual strength and resolve by spending time in God's Word. "I have hidden your word in my heart that I might not sin against you" (Ps. 119:11).

Jesus dealt with temptation decisively and immediately and unapologetically by turning to the authority and promises of Scripture for strength and guidance.

But it is a cliché to say "the devil made me do it." He doesn't make us do anything, he invites us to and we can choose whether or not to accept the invitation.

In high school I played basketball. Our coach would send one of the assistant coaches to scout out the other teams before we played them. Obviously he wanted to know the opponent's strengths and weaknesses, what strategies they might use, and what plays they'd likely turn to late in the game. Then, while we were preparing for the game, our coach would go through a scouting report and we'd study it to try and figure out the best way to defeat our opponent.

The Bible gives us a scouting report on Satan—he's roaming around like a hungry lion looking for people to devour, our pride sets us up for a fall, we fight spiritual warfare with prayer and the shield of faith, defend ourselves with truth and righteousness and the assurance of salvation, and if we resist the devil, he will flee from us (James 4:7).

Scripture explains that our spirits will be willing to follow God's ways, but our old nature is weak. The Bible teaches that sin must be put to death, and we should not become slaves to the old way of life by following our sinful nature but give ourselves to God to be servants of righteousness.

When I think about the things that typically tempt me the most, I have a feeling Satan's scouting report on me would be something like this.

Remember: the most successful tempters work their magic in the dark. The last thing their subjects ever suspect is that they're being tempted at all. We don't want to make Steven afraid, we want to keep him asleep.

Don't forget what you learned in Allurements and Temptations 101 with Dr. Fanglore! Remember his Seven Keys to Keeping Souls Asleep:

1. *Make him very, very comfortable. There's no sedative as strong as the elixir of comfort. Suffering, difficulty, and pain often act as loud alarms for sleeping souls. Never let them go off. It's much better to coddle your subject in comfort than let adversity teach him its lessons.*

2. *Provide constant noise, entertainment, and diversion so he never becomes restless for the real. Keep him distracted—movies, books, internet, Facebook, Twitter, whatever. The distraction doesn't matter, as much as the amount of his time (in other words, his life) that it consumes. Show him the lollipop but don't let him see the needle.*

3. *Selectively remind him of his past. It's best to make sin seem safe beforehand and then fatal afterward. Bury him with shame and guilt and regret. Hopelessness and despair are even better. Let the mistakes of the past be more visible, more defining of his attitude and perspective than the possibilities of the future. As long as he's looking backward he won't be able to look forward to (I hate to even mention the word) heavenly things. Shame! It's all about shame! Despite how commonly we use this technique, he seems*

to keep falling for it. So go back to it as a reliable standby when necessary.

4. *Don't let him think about eternity or how brief his journey across this planet is. Funerals are the strongest wake-up calls of all. Whenever someone he knows dies, do your best to make it tough for him to get to the funeral. Sometimes something as small as a favorite TV show, a traffic jam, or a bad night's sleep can do the trick. As much as possible keep him from thinking about death and the brevity of life. Try to convince him that this day, this moment, couldn't possibly be his last.*

5. *Skew the truth. Relabel sin. Call greed, ambition; self-centeredness, self-esteem; vanity, confidence; lack of faith, practicality. You get the idea.*

6. *Work the weakness angle. This works best with subtle little reminders:*

   - *"You lost your patience last week. You're going to lose it again. You're never going to beat this sin. If God cares so much about you, why doesn't he help you overcome this?"*
   - *"God doesn't love you. If he did he wouldn't have let this happen to you."*
   - *"You're too weak to withstand this." Or its converse: "You're strong enough in your faith. You would never do something like that."*
   - *Or maybe one of the most devastating of all: "God could never love you, not after what you've done."*

7. *Above all, give him whatever he asks for whenever he wants it so he never has to deny himself anything. Once he starts willingly giving up his rights, comforts, or time for what he believes in,*

you're in dangerous territory. As soon as his Christianity costs him something, we've lost the battle.

Of course I don't know if that's what the playbook says about me, but knowing myself as well as I do, if I were a demon who was assigned to tempt Steven James, I'd definitely make sure those topics were covered in-depth.

Take a minute right now, while all of this is fresh in your mind, and jot down some of the things that would appear in a demon's scouting report about you. What plays would he pull out in the fourth quarter when your life is becoming more submissive to God's Spirit?

And how will you rely on the Coach to overcome them?

GOING BACK HOME GOING BACK HOME GOING BACK HOME GOING BACK HOME GOING BACK HOME GOING BACK HOME GOING BACK HOME GOING BACK HOME GOING BACK HOME GOING BACK HOME GOING BACK HOME GOING BACK HOME GOING BACK HOME GOING BACK HOME GOING BACK HOME GOING BACK HOME

9

Going Back Home

The days run together in my mind. A blur of memories and dreams and nightmares that I had no control over. Some days I would be aware of the things I was saying or doing, but often, time would pass in a fog and I'd open my eyes only to realize that days or even a week had swept past.

I lived among the cliffs near the lakeshore in those days and sometimes I'd watch the ships pass, watch the fishermen land. Often they would stare toward the cliffs where I lived; but rarely would they leave their boats. They'd heard the stories of who I was and what I was capable of and so they did not dare ascend those bluffs.

Years ago when I first began experiencing the episodes, I still lived in town. But when the people saw how I would change, witnessed

the things I could do, heard the kind of threats I would make against them and their children, they drove me out.

I ended up living among the tombs that dot the hills here above the lake.

The land of corpses became my home, and in time part of me grew to enjoy the smell of decay.

I had only one change of clothes, filled with lice and maggots that I would eat to save the energy of finding and killing animals for my meals.

At first, men from the city would come to see how I was, to see if I had changed and if the episodes had gone away.

Twice they caught me while I was asleep and chained me, tried to subdue me. But when I awoke and saw them, I felt a surge of terrible strength and yanked against the chains until the blood ran and the chains burst.

The men fled in terror.

When they were gone, the voices within me raged and I turned toward one of the boulders and smashed my face against the stone.

After that, the townspeople stopped coming to check on me.

Often, I would find stones or snap the bones of the corpses and sit for hours slicing at my skin. Narrow red wounds, like mouths, crying out for help that never came.

Everyone hears voices sometimes—the voices of our dreams, our consciences, our desires. Some people say that they can even hear the voice of God. How do we sort them out? How can we tell which ones are coming from ourselves and which might be coming from demons or a deity?

But the things the voices told me to do, I could not imagine any God directing his child to do.

I would roam the hills day and night attacking anyone who got in my way.

Then a month ago on a fog-blurred afternoon when I'd dug up a corpse and was sitting beside it playing with the bones, I sensed something I had never sensed since the episodes began.

Fear.

Looking up, I scanned the hills, an animal's instincts guiding me, rising inside me.

I stood, sniffed the air, but smelled only the lake breeze, carried up the cliffs on a damp wind.

Still, I suspected I'd be able to see the shore from the edge of the cliff. I dropped the bones and rushed toward it.

Yes, fear.

A group of fishermen were halfway up the path and coming my way. I wondered at first if they were lost or if they'd been sent to try and subdue me, but when I saw their leader, a chill shot through me. He was a man who walked with a solid, unhurried gait. I'd never met him, and yet somehow I recognized him.

The voices inside called to me, screamed to me.

Kill him.

It was all I could think of.

Kill him!

But somewhere else, in a part of my heart that'd been buried for far too long, I had the sense that if they were afraid of him I should not be.

I ran toward him.

He watched me, without fear. I was the one who could break out of chains, yet he was the one who was unafraid.

Though the voices were telling me to attack him, they offered me no strength to do it. Amidst their rage I sensed their alarm. And in their fear, I sensed their weakness.

I fell to the ground and one of the voices spoke, using my mouth, a voice trying to sound strong. "What do you want with me, Jesus, Son of the Most High God? Have you come to torture me?"

It was only after the voice spoke his name that I knew who he was. *Jesus.*

This man is Jesus.

Back before the voices began I'd heard of him. A healer. A prophet.

He spoke then, not to me but to whatever lived inside me. He called it an evil spirit and told it to come out.

But nothing changed. I felt the voices cower within me, but they did not leave. They still whispered, still scratched around harsh and vile inside my soul.

Jesus didn't seem surprised that they remained, but then he asked the voice its name.

Then came the cry, not of one but of many—hundreds of shades of darkness all screeching at once, "Legion. We are known as Legion, for we are many."

He looked at me and I sensed he could see inside of me, to both the source of the voices and the center of my heart.

They asked him not to send them out of the area, as if this were their land, this place of death and rot. I wanted to beg him to send them away, far away, to a place where they would never be able to invade another human soul, but instead only their words came out, mine remained muted and unspoken.

"There!" I shouted, but again it wasn't me speaking. My attention went to a herd of pigs nearby. "Send us into the pigs."

He watched me for a moment and maybe he could hear the cry of my heart—the desire that he would set me free from these voices, these forces that controlled me.

"Go," he said simply, and a wind blew through me, a wind that sent them rushing out. As they left, my skin raged as if burned by fire, but the flare of pain eased quickly and a healing warmth embraced me.

And strangely, when all of the voices left, when all of the evil spirits were gone, I didn't feel empty. It was as if when they left, the emptiness left with them.

Embodied with the demons, the pigs rushed at each other in a mad frenzy, then ran for the edge of the cliff and plummeted over, toward the water far below.

At first the fishermen who'd been following Jesus drew back from me, but he assured them that I was fine. One of them ran to the boat and returned with a change of clothes for me.

I slipped them on and went to Jesus. Behind him I saw some of the villagers on their way toward us. Among them I noticed the men who'd been caring for the swine that'd disappeared over the edge of the cliff.

They stared, first at me, then at the man who had set me free, then they shouted warnings to him and to his friends that I was possessed, that they were in danger, but I called out for the villagers to calm down, that I was all right. That he had sent the demons away from me, into the pigs.

In the unsettling wake of my words they begged Jesus to leave.

One of the fishermen carrying a satchel of coins stepped forward and offered payment for the pigs, but the men refused. I had the sense that they didn't care as much about the pigs as they feared Jesus.

He returned to the boat with his friends.

I stared at the people and those gathering beyond them in the town, and I was torn. On the one hand I wanted to go back to my home to my friends and family and show them that I was healed, that I was free, but I also felt drawn to be near this man who had the power to command even demons to obey.

Decide, decide.

You must choose.

As he and his men were climbing aboard their boat, I ran after them and asked him if I could come along and become one of his followers too.

"You don't have to come with me to be my follower."

I didn't understand. "Please, Jesus," I begged. "I need to be—"

He put his hand on my shoulder. "You need to be a husband again to your wife; a father to your children. Your wife and your daughters need you."

"How do you know about . . . ?"

"Go home," he said. "Tell them what I've done for you. Follow me by telling them your story."

He stepped aboard the boat.

"Thank you," I called. The words were so feeble, so weak, so incomplete that I was almost ashamed to use them.

Only after I'd said them did I realize I was crying. And how good it felt to shed tears again.

Then I left to do what he'd said—to follow him by telling the story of all he had done for me. So that others could experience what I finally had.

A new kind of freedom.

A second chance at life.

As Jesus was getting into the boat, the man who had been demon-possessed begged to go with him. Jesus did not let him, but said, "Go home to your family and tell them how much the Lord has done for you, and how he has had mercy on you." So the man went away and began to tell in the Decapolis how much Jesus had done for him. And all the people were amazed. (Mark 5:18–20)

After Jesus set this man free from the control of demons, the ex-demoniac became the first missionary to the Decapolis, ten cities nearby in the region of the Gerasenes.

In modern life, in a society where technology is worshiped and science is king, it's tempting to believe that the world we see is the only world that is. It seems in vogue to try to explain away the miracles of Jesus, to claim that he was too naive or uninformed to know the difference between evil spirits and medical conditions such as epilepsy.

But that's illogical.

Medical conditions are specifically referred to in Scripture, and not everyone who had an evil spirit acted like people suffering from seizures.

In addition, if Jesus was really God, as he claimed to be, then he is certainly powerful enough to command evil spirits what to do. Anyone who can whisper out a world can toss a demon into a pig.

And yet, the temptation to doubt remains.

At times it's easy for us to forget that there is a spiritual, supernatural aspect to life beyond the world we see and touch. Yet the Bible teaches that the supernatural is just as real as the natural. The spirit world is just as present as the material world. When we deny this or live as if it wasn't true, we end up missing out, or sometimes toeing around in the shallows of life rather than diving into its rich depths.

Here is the truth: life is more than you can see and meaning is deeper than this world could ever reveal.

Faith is the ability to see the truth that's invisible. And it involves the act of bending your will toward the unseen. The poet James Hillman put it like this: "Unless his spirit ventures toward the invisible, a man will be unable to perform the daily round with purpose. He will have little joy, only duty—and rebelliousness. The deepest cause of our discontent and of our confused yearnings is the loss of Paradise. . . . The mind wants to break out of the skull and think its way to the stars just as the heart's beat cannot be held in a rib cage."[4]

When the disciples failed to cast out a demon and asked Jesus the reason, he didn't say it was their lack of effort, but their lack of faith (see Matt. 17:19–21). Sometimes I think we need to stop trying so hard and start simply trusting in the things we claim to have faith in.

Don't let the daily grind wipe away your faith in the unseen or your belief in the power of the risen Christ.

Rejoice. Live. Believe.

And tell the story.

Freedom never truly comes until we meet the supernatural and let the one who created it re-create us.

10

Too Late

He didn't come.

We were his friends and he didn't come.

My sister and I had first heard about the Lord through Andrew, and after we met him, we introduced our brother Lazarus to him. Right away, they became fast friends. They would sit for hours talking and laughing and I was so thrilled for Lazarus. Here my brother was, one of the best friends of a healer who was known to be one of the wisest rabbis in the country. And the greatest storyteller we'd ever met.

I still remember the time when Martha, Lazarus, and I arrived on that hill when Jesus was teaching and sharing parables. Clear blue sky the color of the sea, a breeze that whispered across the grass. Jesus finished the illustration he was giving, then lent us a light smile and began another story, this time about a man named Lazarus.

A few people who knew us looked our way, but Lazarus shrugged off the attention. Jesus was describing a poor man, a beggar who lived outside a rich man's home, and that wasn't my brother at all.

But still.

I found it odd that Jesus should use his name since the Lord had never mentioned anyone by name in his parables before.

Jesus went on to explain that the rich man lived in luxury, and with the finest clothes and food and the most influential friends.

But outside his gate there was a man named Lazarus who was infected with sores, lonely, and had only wild dogs as his companions.

Apparently, the rich man would walk past him daily to enter and leave his home, but he just ignored Lazarus.

Even though I assumed it was a parable, it might just as well have been a story from real life because whether or not it was true, it happened all the time. We saw the rich ignore the poor every day in our towns.

Jesus went on to explain that both of the men died. The rich man, whom Jesus didn't name, was buried and arrived in hell, but Lazarus was carried by the angels to Abraham's side. The rich man suffered greatly and in time he looked up, across a great gulf, and saw Abraham with Lazarus beside him.

And then everything from the first part of the story was tipped on its head—the rich man was now alone, the lonely man was now in community; the man who'd been outside the gate was within, the man who'd been inside his home was cast out; the man who'd been hungry was provided for, the man who'd had everything had nothing; the man who'd suffered was comforted, the man who'd been comfortable was suffering; the man with great longing was satisfied, the man who'd been satisfied with this world longed to be comforted in the next.

Everything reversing itself at the moment of death.

"The rich man," Jesus said, "begged Abraham to send·Lazarus to dip his finger in water and cool his tongue."

And I remember staring at Jesus in unbelief. Could it be that even after all that had happened the rich man still thought only of himself? Was he still treating Lazarus like he would treat a servant, asking Abraham to have him run errands for him?

Perhaps.

Jesus didn't clarify, but he did explain that Abraham pointed out the obvious, the irony that ran through the narrative: "In your lifetime you had good things, Lazarus had bad, but now he is being comforted and you are in agony. In addition, because of the great gulf between you and us, no one can travel from your region to ours, and our region to yours."

But the rich man wouldn't give up. Once again he asked Abraham to have Lazarus do his bidding. "Have him tell my five brothers about this place so that they will not also come here."

The hillside was silent. Jesus took a long, slow breath, then said softly, "And Abraham told him, 'They have the testimony of Moses and the prophets. That is enough for anyone. It's enough for them, whether they listen to it or not. It is enough.'" He paused, then added, "It's always enough."

And the rich man, who was no longer rich in any way, argued with Abraham that if someone from the dead were to rise and go to them, they would repent. Jesus said, "But Abraham replied that if they would not repent from hearing the words of God proclaimed, they would neither believe nor repent, even if someone rose from the dead."

As the Lord told the story, the day seemed to become chillier. The story itself was shocking enough. Everyone I knew believed that the rich were blessed and the poor, the afflicted, were being punished by God for past sins.

But Jesus's story contradicted that.

Just like nearly all of Jesus's stories, it didn't have a happy ending for all the people in the story. Instead, it was another deep warning dressed up as a tale: be rich in the ways of the spirit even if you are poor in the ways of the world. And believe now, while you still have the chance to change.

It was very sudden, Lazarus's illness. Jesus was in a town across the Jordan so we sent word right away that he was sick. We figured that Jesus would come, that whatever he was doing he would come right away.

But he didn't. We waited and watched for him, but he didn't come.

My brother died.

Two days passed.

A third.

And by the time Jesus arrived, Lazarus had been in the tomb for four days.

I remember feeling hot anger, a heart full of disappointment in Jesus. When your friends are in need, when they're sick unto death, you come to be with them. To comfort them.

That's what you do for the people you care about. You don't abandon them when they need you most.

That's what I thought.

That's what I felt like saying to everyone who had come to mourn my brother's passing.

Bethany is only a couple miles from Jerusalem, and that's where many of our friends live, so there were lots of people here at the house that day. When they saw Jesus approaching, some of them went out to meet him. Martha joined them, then hurried ahead of them.

I stayed in the house.

A few minutes later I found out that Martha had asked him why he didn't come sooner. No kind words, no greeting, no small talk. Classic Martha—just the blunt observation, "If you would have been here, he wouldn't have died. But even now I know that whatever you will, God will grant."

Admirable faith lay in those words, but also a rebuke for Jesus. Even as she reaffirmed how much she believed in his power, she was questioning his motives for taking his time. And then his reply: "I am the rising from the dead; I am life. Whoever lives believing in me will never die; and whoever dies believing in me will live forever. Do you believe this?"

"Yes," Martha said. "I believe."

That's when she came to me and quickly summarized the conversation. After she was done she told me that the Teacher was asking to see me.

I rushed out, a raging disappointment in my heart. As soon as I reached him I dropped to my knees, bowed my head to the ground. "Lord, if only you had been here Lazarus would not have died."

If.

If you had been here.

But you weren't.

I tried to hold back my tears, but failed. I wept at his feet, and when he spoke I could hear deep emotion in his voice. "Where did you lay him?"

The others showed him the grave. I followed, unable to find any words. But then I noticed Jesus wipe away a tear and heard someone near me whisper words that echoed my thoughts—if he loved his friend so much, why didn't he come sooner? If he could cure a blind man, certainly he could have helped to heal Lazarus. The least he could have done was show up.

The least he could have done.

I'd thought his love was deep. But how can there be depth of concern when you abandon someone in his time of greatest need?

Jesus approached the tomb, a small cave cut into the rock where we'd placed my brother's body. A boulder had been rolled in front of the entrance to keep out the dogs and other scavengers.

"Roll away the stone," Jesus said.

For a moment no one moved. "He's been in there four days," Martha replied softly. "His body is returning to the earth. The smell will be—"

"Roll it away."

At last they did, and the sour smell of death seeped out into the day. People eased back, the women sliding their headscarves over their faces to shield themselves from the smell.

Then Jesus called, "Lazarus, come out."

We stared at the Lord, then at the entrance. No one spoke. My heart was hammering with disbelief and a whisper of hope. Could he be serious? Truly, calling my brother—

"Come out, Lazarus," he repeated.

Then.

The smell of death evaporated.

A wisp of fresh air fluttered past us.

And when I saw movement in the shadows of the cave I felt myself grow weak. My brother appeared and my knees buckled beneath me. Then Jesus, the man who'd been overcome with grief only moments earlier, now looked like he might burst out laughing. "Get him out of those grave clothes!"

I waited only long enough for Lazarus to be clothed, and then I threw my arms around him. His skin held no hint of the stench of the grave, only a sweet fragrance that seemed like the scent of heaven itself.

The words the Lord had spoken to my sister rang in my mind: "Whoever dies believing in me will live forever. Do you believe this?"

Yes, my Lord.

I do.

Now, at last, I know that I do.

The sisters sent word to Jesus, "Lord, the one you love is sick."

When he heard this, Jesus said, "This sickness will not end in death. No, it is for God's glory so that God's Son may be glorified through it." (John 11:3–4)

Christianity is a strange religion.

Believe.

Receive.

Suffer.

Rejoice.

Evangelists are usually good at explaining the first two; after all, John wrote, "To all who received him, to those who believed in his name, he gave the right to become children of God" (1 John 1:12).

And the final rejoicing part is usually pretty well represented in sermons too.

But number three? Suffer? Is that really part of the deal?

Right after being stoned and left for dead, Paul took his friend Barnabas to Lystra, Iconium, and Antioch, "strengthening the disciples and encouraging them to remain true to the faith. 'We must go through many hardships to enter the kingdom of God,' they said" (Acts 14:22).

I find Paul's message a very informative one-sentence sermon.

Hardship is part of the journey to the kingdom. Paul cycled back to this idea time after time:

> If we are to share his glory, we must also share his suffering. Yet what we suffer now is nothing compared to the glory he will reveal to us later. For all creation is waiting eagerly for that future day when God will reveal who his children really are. (Rom. 8:17–19 NLT)

> You can be sure that the more we suffer for Christ, the more God will shower us with his comfort through Christ. (2 Cor. 1:5)

> As a result, I can really know Christ and experience the mighty power that raised him from the dead. I can learn what it means to suffer with him, sharing in his death. (Phil. 3:10)

The difference between perseverance and endurance is that when you persevere it's for a reason. You have hope for the future, meaning of some kind that you're pursuing. But those who simply endure have no hope and no ultimate reason to keep them going beyond the instinctual desire for survival. They see no meaning in their pain, so consequently, the exact same experiences are experienced differently by different people simply because of one small four letter word that changes everything. Hope.

The moment you give up hope you are lost.

Believe.

Receive.

Suffer.

Rejoice.

Lazarus, his family and friends all suffered, but Jesus had a plan bigger than his suffering to put into play—the rejoicing part.

No one else understood at first, but God was glorified in the end.

In a startling paradox, the most dangerous thing of all isn't to suffer but *not to* suffer. As C. S. Lewis noted, "Security is mortals' greatest enemy."[5] This is because safety, comfort, and security are all sleeping potions. They subtly soak into my daily life and sedate my soul. Danger, on the other hand, wakes me up. Pain screams in my ear.

As it turns out, since self-indulgence is the sedative for my heart, and the more I take, the less likely it becomes that I'll ever wake up. Suffering is the alarm clock for my soul.

God tries to awaken me. The ship has hit the iceberg, and it's going down, but I'm fast asleep in my berth dreaming reasonable dreams. But because he loves me, he shakes me awake. And sometimes that means slapping me in the face. After all, he's willing to risk everything to give me the chance to be rescued.

The question of suffering is impossible to understand unless we look at it within the bigger context of eternity.

Jesus was informed that Pilate had murdered some people from Galilee as they were sacrificing at the Temple in Jerusalem. "Do you think those Galileans were worse sinners than other people from Galilee?" he asked. "Is that why they suffered? Not at all! And you will also perish unless you turn from your evil ways and turn to God. And what about the eighteen men who died when the Tower of Siloam fell on them? Were they the worst sinners in Jerusalem? No, and I tell you again that unless you repent, you will also perish." (Luke 13:1–5)

Jesus had the chance to get God off the hook once and for all with this question of evil, but he seems to only redirect the argument from focusing on God to focusing on us.

It's as if Jesus is saying, "Death ain't the worst thing that can happen to you, amigo. Spending your life going your way rather than mine, is."

To Jesus, the main issue is not why does evil exist, but rather, how will you live while you wait for the answer? Will you believe in the law and the prophets or get sucked into self-centeredness like the rich man?

Sometimes God's plan is woven through pain, and his glory is revealed in ways we would never anticipate, as it was in Mary's case when she saw her brother come back from the dead.

We tend to think that the worst thing that could happen to us is to suffer misfortune, tragedy, unanswered prayers, or death. But in truth, the worst thing that could happen is that we don't become more like Jesus.

There is a purpose deeply hidden, even in our pain.

Even in sickness.

Even in death.

God allows us to make the choice between safe but fatal skepticism or dangerous but life-giving faith. Real life lies on the edge of a dare.

Turning to thoughts of eternity, of God's glory and our ultimate home, serve as the best remedy for regaining perspective when we're in the midst of painful situations and troubling questions. And it is the best remedy when we're tempted to question God.

Those who settle in here have invested their future in the wrong place.

Believe.

Receive.

Suffer.

Rejoice forever.

11

The Dreamer

Sometimes God whispers to me in a place beneath my senses. He speaks in a way I can't touch or smell or taste, with words I can't hear with my ears and with truths I can't see with my eyes. Call them visions, spiritual experiences, whatever you wish. I call them dreams.

And the ones I had last night will always haunt me.

A man beaten.

A man scourged.

Crucified.

But the man was innocent.

And my husband was the killer.

I hurried from my private quarters to find my husband, but he was already stationed before the people.

From where I stood I could look out across the courtyard, could see him seated at the top of the grand stone steps, the Jews spread before him at the bottom. Not only did the raised throne exalt my husband, it made it easier for him to make his proclamations, to be heard by the hundreds of people who would gather to hear if prisoners had been condemned or freed. Exclamations of life and death, condemnation or pardon. Pontius held destiny in his hands and he enjoyed the feeling.

The man whom I had dreamed about was standing on the platform near my husband, flanked by two soldiers. I recognized him from the dream.

He'd been beaten and now stood wrapped in a cheap purple robe, a bloodstained mockery of royalty. A circle of woven thorns had been pushed onto his head.

I stood there petrified.

This is the man. He is innocent!

I asked a servant beside me what was happening and he told me the man was a prophet who'd been accused of crimes against the empire.

"A prophet?"

"The Jews claim he is trying to start a rebellion against Caesar."

But the Jews want their freedom so bad that if this man really were leading an uprising, they wouldn't have been handing him over to be killed, they would be hiding him away to plan their insurrection.

Then the servant added, "The man claims to be a Son of God."

When he said that I recognized the prophet as the man who'd entered Jerusalem less than a week earlier to the cries and shouts of "Hosanna!" The people had cried out that their king had arrived riding on a donkey, yet not just their king, but their Lord.

He's innocent!

Something more was going on here, it was obvious.

"They could not get him to speak," the servant told me in a rushed whisper. "All morning he has been quiet. Even as they beat him. Even as they tortured him."

This made me even more uneasy. My husband's soldiers are well-schooled in the art of getting people to talk. Everyone confesses eventually—even the innocent—it's just a matter of time.

But this prophet had said nothing and even now, as I looked at him surveying the crowd, I did not see the eyes of a broken man. What kind of a person can withstand beatings like that and still stand unashamed, unafraid, with a stillness as deep as the sea?

I could tell that the man's silence was taking its toll on my husband.

So Pontius tried to appeal to a loophole. Since it was a special religious holiday for the Jews, he would typically release one of the prisoners to them. It was his way of appeasing them, a small gift to earn their allegiance. So now he quieted the crowd with a raised hand and shouted, "Which of the two do you want me to release to you? Barabbas or this Jesus, whom people call the Messiah?"

As a woman, decorum, as well as the law, forbade me from entering the courtyard and speaking with my husband directly. So I scribbled a note and sent it with the servant even before the people could reply. "Hurry!" I cried to the servant. "This must not go on."

While the crowd murmured I saw Pontius unfold my note.

And this is what I wrote: "Have nothing to do with this innocent man. Last night I suffered much in a dream because of him."

Some of the people began shouting for the prophet to die. Some were waving their fists in the air.

I watched Pontius. He didn't look toward me. He just stared at the note for a moment, as if he were trying to figure out what to do next.

At last he gazed at the crowd again and repeated, "Who do you want me to release to you?"

No, no. Pontius. Please.

The answer to his question was obvious, they wanted Jesus killed.

"Barabbas," shouted a few men.

Then the response crescendoed into a chant. "Barabbas! Barabbas!" The loudest voices drowned out the quieter bystanders until they too joined in and the cry of the crowd filled the courtyard. "Barabbas!"

My husband seemed stunned by their response. "Then what do you want me to do with Jesus?"

A single voice replied first, his words sharp and hateful and cold. "Crucify him!" As he repeated his cry, others followed suit, the crowd finally shouting as one, "Crucify him! Crucify him!"

They shouted even louder for this innocent man's death than they had for the guilty man's pardon.

"But why!" yelled my husband. I heard him, though the crowd kept shouting, trying to drown out his voice. At last their cries trickled away into a taut silence. "Why?" Pontius said. "What law has he broken? What crime has he committed?"

They gave no reasons. They offered no explanation, only yelled louder, "Crucify him! Crucify him!" A macabre chant calling for the death of an innocent man. "Crucify! Crucify!" The word rose, shuddered, thundered through the crowd.

And echoed somberly inside of me. A riot was forming. The people were grabbing rocks and sticks, anything that was nearby.

But my husband raised his hand and the writhing crowd quieted enough for him to address them.

Yes, yes, tell them you will not kill an innocent man.

He glanced in my direction, but only briefly. Then he called for a basin of water and a towel.

"So be it," he announced to the crowd.

No, Please! I almost said the words aloud. *Don't have anything to do with this mocking of justice. He is innocent!*

By the time the water arrived, Pontius had regained his self-composure and he spoke in a firm voice, resolute. One at a time he dipped his hands into the basin and rinsed them. "Then I wash my hands of this man's blood. I am innocent of his death. It is your responsibility. It is on your hands."

"Yes," someone called. Then another added, "Let his blood fall on us. Let his guilt land on us and our children."

And then, my husband acquiesced to them. He released Barabbas, a guilty man, though he knew him to be guilty; he condemned an innocent man, though he knew him to be innocent.

They led the prophet out and I felt a rise of terror in my heart.

I felt the guilt of the day fall on me and I wanted to run to the prophet and ask him to forgive me for failing to save him.

If only I'd sent the note sooner, or written more urgency into it. If only I'd done more, this innocent man, the Jewish Messiah, would still be alive.

I wished there really was some way to wash off the regrets, to wash off the guilt. That's what I was thinking as they led him away. Though not a Jew, I called out to the Jewish God, *O God of Jacob, if you are there, find a way to save him. You sent me the dream, now find a way to give him life. O God, if you're there.*

And now as I watch the prophet die on the cross, his blood dripping to the ground, I wonder if there is a way, any way at all, to wash away the blood of a guilty conscience. To make it unblemished once again.

While Pilate was sitting on the judge's seat, his wife sent him this message: "Don't have anything to do with that innocent man, for I have suffered a great deal today in a dream because of him."

But the chief priests and the elders persuaded the crowd to ask for Barabbas and to have Jesus executed. (Matt. 27:19–20)

This is a fascinating story for me, partly because it's so often dropped out of modern Good Friday or Easter services, sermons, and messages. It also intrigues me because we know so few of the details: God sent a dream, or at the very least, allowed Claudia to have one, that reiterated Jesus's innocence. But that's all we know—and yet she took action. She had little proof, but she acted on the little that she knew about Jesus's innocence, the little that God had revealed to her.

The disciples fled, but this Roman governor's wife tried to save Jesus's life.

There were a number of people who, during the last hours of his life (or just after his death), recognized that Jesus was truly an innocent man—Pontius Pilate, Judas, one of the soldiers watching the crucifixion, and Claudia. Presumably the apostles and the rest of Jesus's followers did as well, although we're not specifically told that in Scripture.

At one point Jesus challenged the religious leaders to find anything wrong with his life, any discrepancies between his message and his life (John 8:46), and they couldn't come up with anything.

What would it be like to watch a man whom you know to be innocent suffer the death penalty?

I know this to be true: He is innocent; I am not. This is one of the central aspects of the gospel message. But the gospel is working on me. When we're responsive to God's guiding he'll shape us, change us. As soon as we stop resisting him.

Yes, we all give in to temptation and, in a sense, all of us bear some responsibility for the death of Jesus, but the very blood we caused to be spilled is the blood that washes us clean.

Since we have now been justified by his blood, how much more shall we be saved from God's wrath through him! (Rom. 5:9)

That is the message that washes off the guilt.
That finally makes a conscience unblemished once again.

WAKING THE DEAD
WAKING THE DEAD
WAKING THE DEAD
WAKING THE DEAD
WAKING THE DEAD
WAKING THE DEAD
WAKING THE DEAD
WAKING THE DEAD
WAKING THE DEAD
WAKING THE DEAD
WAKING THE DEAD
WAKING THE DEAD
WAKING THE DEAD
WAKING THE DEAD
WAKING THE DEAD

12

Waking the Dead

It isn't the blood that bothers me the most. Or even the smell. It's seeing the families when the moment comes. That's always the toughest part.

Sometimes they just can't stop screaming. Sometimes they shake as one wave of tears after another grabs hold of them. Sometimes they pound the walls. They cling to each other. They collapse on the floor. They get that lost look in their eyes and just stand there trembling. Powerless. Hopeless.

From that first ear-piercing wail to the tired, tearless, bloodshot eyes, it's the hardest part of my job.

Sometimes the little kids laugh. They don't understand. "He's only sleeping, Mommy," they say. "Don't worry. He'll wake up." They're too young to comprehend what has happened.

Most adults can't accept it right away either. They deny it. They convince themselves it's all some kind of mistake. They pretend it's not real. And then suddenly, the realization sinks in. The light drains out of their eyes. And this terrible, stretching loneliness seeps in.

When I see that, I have to look away.

Even though I'm not twenty yet, I've been through it all dozens of times because it's my job to be there. To help the family grieve.

Ever since I was a little girl, I've had an ear for music. When my mother noticed it, back when I was about five, she arranged for me to take flute lessons.

At weddings I play tunes of joy. At funerals I play songs of pain.

The families always walk us past the corpse so we can see it for ourselves, so we can give a clearer voice to their grief. That's never easy either.

I especially hate it when it's kids.

I always look at them, thinking, *She was only eight . . . or ten . . . or two . . . You've already lived ten years or eight years or sixteen years longer than she ever will . . . That could've been you laying there, Aaliyah . . . That could've been you . . .*

Then I close my eyes and lift my flute to my lips. And I begin to play. The music fills the room. The mourners join the song. The whisper of my flute and the pain of their cries blend together into a lament that lets everyone in the town know what has happened.

Some of the mourners are family members, of course. But if the family is rich enough, they'll hire professional mourners to help comfort them, to give voice to their grief.

Weeping. Wailing. Crying. Shouting. Sometimes they'll tear their clothes apart, pull their own hair out, or smear ashes on their face to show the depth of their grief. We don't hide pain around here.

I guess in some cultures it might seem odd to make such a public display of our grief. But not to us. Instead of wearing black or hiding our tears or speaking in hushed tones, we let loose. We let our sorrow slash through us and land in the streets. We don't secrete death away here.

But still the mourners and musicians don't really feel the family's grief. I mean, of course we're sad. But it's one thing to cry, and it's another to grieve. You can pay someone to cry in front of you, but you can't hire her to feel your loss. You can pay someone to play a song for you, but you can't hire her to know your heart. Crying is one thing. Grieving is another. Grieving is something you have to do alone.

So a few months ago I was preparing lunch with my mother when the door burst open. The messenger was out of breath. "Jairus asked for you," the man gasped. "Before going to find the healer, he asked for you. She's not getting any better. You might be needed." He paused and then added, "Right away."

I nodded slowly. My mother lowered her eyes.

The messenger was from the family of the ruler of our synagogue. Jairus was the kind of man who would sit with families in their time of loss, praying and fasting for them. And he would never complain about it. But now it was his daughter who was sick—his only daughter.

Over the last two weeks every time she seemed to be getting better, every time the family got their hopes up again, the fever would return worse than before.

In the last couple of days her breathing had become ragged and weak. All of us knew she wouldn't last long.

I'd been expecting this. I laid down the dough I was kneading and wiped off my hands. Mother was used to me leaving like this; she knew what it meant. I grabbed my flute and headed for the door.

As I approached the house, I could hear the mourners shrieking with sorrow. Their cries told me all I needed to know.

I found out almost immediately that Jairus didn't even know what had happened yet. As I walked in the door, two servants were leaving to tell him. I guess they were hoping to find him before he brought the healer over.

So while they went to look for the father, the hired mourners and I went to look at the girl.

I walked up the stairs slowly. I could hear the mother and a few of the women in the room at the top of the stairs. Their wails ripped through me. So hopeless. So raw. So fierce with pain. There's nothing as heartbreaking as the sound of a mother's cry when she kneels beside her dead child. It is always sharper than that of the women she hires to mourn with her.

Quietly, I entered the room and looked at the girl. Her eyes were closed. Her chest was still, her face pale. I knew that if I touched her hand, it would feel like cool meat and not warm flesh. I knew because back when I first began playing at funerals, I would touch the hands just to make sure. But I stopped doing that long ago. The feel of cold clay would haunt me.

I don't touch the hands anymore.

I'd heard she was twelve, but she was small for her age. Her dark hair hung still and thick, cascading off her mat and onto the floor like a thin black waterfall. Frozen in time. Frozen in death.

A lump rose in my throat.

Oh how I hate it when it's children.

As I looked at the body, I saw a crimson bead oozing out of the corner of her mouth. No one else had seen it yet. I couldn't stand the thought of the mother looking up and seeing that rose-red blood staining her daughter's face. So I gently wiped the dead girl's mouth with the sleeve of my tunic and placed my other hand on the shoulder of the shaking, crumpled mother to try and comfort her, but it doesn't seem to work. Her sobs didn't quiet down.

Then, with the dead girl's blood drying on my sleeve, I went back downstairs with the others. I pulled out my flute and began to play a song full of tears and blood and death. It was one of the saddest songs I'd ever played.

We'd been at it for almost an hour when they arrived.

I saw them approaching through the window: Jairus, the servants, the healer and some of his followers, all silently walking up to the door.

I decided the healer had probably come to offer a prayer, or perhaps to console the family.

As he entered the house and saw us, his voice rose above the cries of even the loudest mourners. "Stop. Quiet! What are you doing?"

I eased the flute from my lips and looked around. Slowly, the sound of weeping died down until all was silent in the house. Everyone was staring at him.

"This girl isn't dead," he said firmly. "She's only asleep."

The room was silent for a moment longer, but that was all. Then one of the younger mourners made a sound. It started as a snicker in the back of the room, then spread among the mourners, a series of giggles, a ripple of laughter. Not the clean kind of laughter you let out after a good joke, but the rotten kind of laughter that seeps out when the joke isn't funny at all.

I'm ashamed to admit it, but I laughed with the others. Softly, not as loud as some of them, but I laughed too. We knew that Jairus's daughter wasn't asleep. The girl was dead.

Immediately, I felt a rush of shame for laughing and held back.

The parents and servants didn't laugh. They stood there in shock, quivering slightly. They didn't laugh. No, of course they didn't laugh. Love would never have let them. But the women with me weren't being paid to love the girl, just to help the family grieve for her.

But in that tragic, horrible moment we laughed.

"Get out of here." The rabbi threw open the door with a bang. "All of you, get out!" Then he pointed to a few of his friends. "You, Peter, John, James. Come with me."

But the girl is dead. What's he doing . . . ?

"Outside," he repeated. "Now."

Some of the other mourners had set their jaws. Some were sneering. But slowly, they began to file out the door.

I didn't know what to do. Finally, I set my flute on a shelf near the stairs so I could find it easily when he let us back in to finish our work, then I stepped outside into the late afternoon sunlight to wait with the others.

For a few minutes some of the girls kept giggling until one of the older ladies shushed them. Someone said something about how she better still get paid. Then it was pretty much quiet.

None of the mourners were crying anymore.

What is he doing in there? Why bring the healer here when the girl is already dead? And why on earth would he say she was only asleep?

"Huh!" one lady announced suddenly. "Does he want I should stand around here all day?" She looked around for support. "I'm going home."

Another woman nodded. "If he wants to make jokes about a dead girl, I'm going home too."

But he hadn't been joking. From his tone, from the look on his face, that much I knew.

The crowd of mourners began to shrink as the women headed home.

I just stood there. Should I wait or go? The sound of our sour laughter echoed in my head. I was ashamed, but what could I do?

Nothing.

I couldn't do anything. The girl was dead, and the healer didn't want us here. I didn't want to look him in the eye, not after laughing with the others, so I decided to go back home and help my mother finish baking the bread.

But I couldn't leave without my flute. I had to go back in and get it.

They're upstairs. Just be quiet. Be quick.

I eased the door open and stepped inside. It took a moment for my eyes to adjust to the dim light. The house was eerily silent. It didn't even sound like the parents were crying upstairs.

I crossed the room softly, and just as I reached for my flute, I heard a loud gasp from upstairs.

Then a shout.

Then a squeal of surprise, of terrible joy.

"Daughter. My daughter!" It was the voice of the dead girl's mother. "You're back. You're alive!"

What?

A moment later a cluster of people emerged from the room at the top of the stairs.

And as they did, a chill trickled down my spine.

No. It can't be.

A ghost. The ghost of the girl floating beside her father.

No!

My eyes were playing tricks on me. My eyes had to be playing tricks on me!

I staggered backward, clutching my flute.

She saw me. "Shalom!" the girl called. *Peace!*

Ghosts don't smile and wish you blessings and peace.

"Shalom!" she said again. And I knew she was no ghost. She waved at me. The girl I'd been hired to help mourn was coming down the stairs.

I mouthed the word, "Shalom," but no sound came out.

The healer's three friends were staring at me from the top of the stairs. The girl's mother and father were there too. All of them looked as stunned as I felt. Then Jesus, the healer, stepped out of the room and looked at me.

"I . . . I forgot my flute," I whispered. I thought he would almost certainly be angry at me for coming back into the house. "I'm sorry. I didn't—"

"It's all right," he said softly. "But you mustn't tell anyone what you saw." Then he gazed around the room. "Any of you. Do you understand? You must not tell a soul."

I nodded slowly. So did the others.

He pointed at me. "Promise me. Not a word."

"I . . . I . . ."

"Promise me."

"I promise," I said.

"Good. Now go on home, Aaliyah. And not a word, even to your mother."

What? How does he know your name? How does he know your mother?

I nodded. I couldn't keep my eyes off the girl.

And as I backed out the front door, I heard Jesus laugh a little—a clear, clean laugh. "Jairus, give your daughter something to eat. The time for mourning is over."

As I stepped into the afternoon sunlight, everything seemed surreal. Like a dream. The funeral. The girl. Maybe I was asleep. Maybe that was it. Maybe I was dreaming . . .

Then I noticed the sleeve of my dress smeared with a dead girl's blood; a dead girl who was no longer dead. I touched the dried blood. It was real. It was all real.

I was frightened but also filled with a terrible kind of awe at the healer.

People had been saying that he had come from God, from heaven itself . . . and there was no other explanation. He must have. How else could he have done it?

A rush of excitement, and I thought, *You have to tell someone. You have to tell everyone!*

But I'd promised not to say a word.

As much as I told myself to keep quiet, in the end I couldn't help it. I didn't keep the promise I'd made to the healer.

I just couldn't keep the news to myself. How could I not tell the story? And it wasn't just me. As soon as the other women who'd been there saw the girl at the market the next day, word spread like wildfire and the whole town knew. The whole region did. Jesus had brought a dead girl back to life.

And we had laughed at him when he went in to awaken her.

It bothered me that I hadn't kept my promise to him. At first I didn't understand why he'd told us to be quiet. It didn't make any sense to me.

At first.

But then, as time wore on and his reputation grew, he had to start avoiding the crowds. He had to stop teaching in some areas altogether. I began to see that fame wasn't what he wanted. Popularity was his enemy. Then the angry politicians and rulers rose against him. They claimed he was a threat to our religion and our way of life. Things were spinning out of control. His notability was strangling his ministry. And I knew I was partly to blame. First I'd laughed at him. Then I'd failed him. And now he was in trouble.

I remember thinking, *What have I done?*

How I wanted to apologize! But of course I didn't get a chance to talk to him. Then came his trial . . . his conviction . . . his crucifixion.

I never got the chance to say I was sorry. And I couldn't help but feel that it was partly my fault that he was hanging there, dying on that cross. After all, I'd done the opposite of what he wanted, what he asked of me. And they'd caught him, and now they were killing him.

This man who could awaken the dead was dying.

The politicians and priests laughed at him as he hung there struggling for breath.

I recognized their kind of laughter.

I cried that day—real tears, not manufactured ones. I was grieving then. For real.

The sun itself seemed to die, and as darkness swept over the land, I saw his mother kneeling at the foot of the cross, crying before the cooling corpse of her son.

A mother's cry. The fiercest pain of all.

No one was asked to play a flute at his death. No one was hired to mourn.

I climb the hill and look around. Lots of other people are already gathered. Dozens of us, hundreds, maybe. All waiting expectantly. I take my flute with me. Habit.

I'm trembling slightly, filled with a strange mixture of fear and hope. Fear because I feel guilty. And hope that maybe, just maybe, the story I've heard is true.

The rumors have been circulating for a couple of weeks now. Here's what we know for sure—they buried him, sealed the tomb, and set a guard. But during the weekend the body disappeared. No one knew where it was. And within a few days his followers were telling people they'd seen him again. Alive. Back from the dead.

So now, on this day, we've gathered. To see for ourselves.

Jairus and his daughter are here. She's laughing and running with her friends and smiling and letting the sunlight dance across her face.

She waves to me.

"Shalom!"

"Shalom," I say.

"You came to play for me!" she says. "When I died!" And I don't know what to say. I want to tell her that I laughed about her death, but I can't seem to. I want to say I'm sorry that I spread the news, that I played my part in sending her healer to die, but I don't.

"Yes," I say at last, waving my flute in her direction, doing my best to sound happy. "I played for you when you died."

A moment later the day around me splits open.

And as we gasp, he appears.

We drop to our knees, but he tells us to get up. We want to bow at his feet, but he opens his arms to hug us one at a time instead. The children are the first ones to run to him. They're not afraid.

But I am. I wait. I hide in the back of the crowd.

But his eyes find me.

"I know you," he says. And he invites me forward. "Come here, Aaliyah."

I'm afraid to approach him, but I do. He draws me into his arms. He is no ghost. He is real.

I'm shaking. I know what I have to say. But I struggle with the words. Fear chokes me. It takes me three tries.

"I laughed," I say at last.

"I know," he says.

"And I told. I know you didn't want me to tell, but I did. I couldn't keep it to myself."

"I know."

The moment weighs heavily on me. I want so badly for him to accept me even though I've let him down.

Finally, I manage to get out the words that've been tearing away at my soul. "I'm so sorry," I whisper. By then I'm crying.

"Yes, I know. But I don't want your regrets," he says, "only your peace."

Then he takes both of my hands and looks me in the eyes. His hands aren't cool like clay—they're warm and invitingly alive. "I'm not angry with you, Aaliyah." He wipes my tears away, touching my cheek as softly as a melody. "This time you can tell." His voice is somehow calm but also filled with urgency. "This time I want you to tell. Tell everyone."

"Tell them?"

"Yes. The story. It's time they heard."

"Oh, Rabbi," I stammer, "I will."

And this time I'll keep my promise. I really will. I'll share the news, the mystery of it all. I'll tell his story and play the song of life so even those who weren't there that day can meet him for themselves. So they can meet the living, breathing Mystery for themselves, for he didn't just awaken that girl. He didn't just awaken himself. He also awakened me.

"And now," he says with a wide grin. "Before I go home, how about a little song? Something lively. Something we can really dance to."

I nod and lift my flute to my lips.

And I begin to play.

When Jesus entered the ruler's house and saw the flute players and the noisy crowd, he said, "Go away. The girl is not dead but asleep." But they laughed at him. After the crowd had been put outside, he went in and took the girl by the hand, and she got up. News of this spread through all that region. (Matt. 9:23–26)

A fable

I had a dream that I was a block of marble.

As the sculptor picked up the hammer and chisel I thought, *No, put those down . . . don't press that sharp chisel against my surface!*

But he approached me and placed its tip against my face. And he began to chip away at my surface.

I saw pieces of myself fall to his feet.

He moved slowly from my head to my chest. And then to my arms and my legs. He worked carefully, until at last, I was no longer just a block of marble, but I had the form and shape and likeness of a man.

Yet, I was still only a statue.

And then he did a strange thing.

The sculptor leaned close to me. He looked into my unblinking eyes, and then he breathed on me. And his spirit, the spirit of my creator, passed across my stony skin.

In that moment, my heart—no longer a heart of stone, but one of flesh and blood—began to beat. Blood coursed through my limbs and breath filled my lungs.

I was no longer a statue.

I was a man.

Slowly, I flexed my fingers and looked at the shape of my arm. Then my torso and my legs. I realized that I didn't look anything like the thing I used to be, but I looked like the person I was meant to be all along.

The sculptor took my hand. "Welcome to my world."

As I stepped off the pedestal, I gazed at the pieces of myself scattered across the floor. "What are you going to do with those?"

"Leave 'em here."

But they'd been a part of me for so long; I didn't want to leave them behind. I wanted to pick them up and take them with me and glue them back onto myself.

"You're no longer a sculpture," he said. "You're a person—flesh and breath and love and dreams. Those are only pieces of stone. They belong here. Come on."

It hurt leaving them behind, but I followed him and with each step they seemed to matter to me less and less.

As we walked toward the door I glanced at the mirror on the wall and I saw that the face the sculptor had given me was his own. His likeness was etched upon my likeness so that I would carry his image into the world.

He pressed open the door and led me into the daylight of the world.

And I awoke from the dream and realized it was more than a dream. It was the story of my life.

Day by day, moment by moment, the chisel falls against my surface. I don't know precisely what I'll look like when God is eventually done with me. But I do know that I'll no longer look like I do now, that I'll become more like I was meant to be all along. "Yes, dear friends, we are already God's children, and we can't even imagine what we will be like when Christ returns. But we do know that when he comes we will be like him, for we will see him as he really is" (1 John 3:2).

Yet, even with that promise, sometimes I can't help but question the pieces of my life God decides to chip away.

Daily, I struggle to trust the Sculptor and stop fighting against the blows that leave the parts of myself that I used to believe were so essential, scattered at my feet or blown away in a puff of dusty breeze. And the thought of actually welcoming the chisel—that's too much for me.

It hurts terribly to see huge chunks of my ego and pride fall away. But I'm finally beginning to understand that's how God transforms us into his own likeness. That, and the gentle breath of his Spirit blowing against the surface of my life. Blowing the dust away.

> I complain about the
> chisel only because I don't
> have the mind of the sculptor.
> I don't know what I will become in his hands.
> Or what I will look like
> when he is finished
>   with his harsh artistry.
> Until then, my pain will never fully
> make sense.

New life from old.

New hope from bitter tears. And victory from the darkest failure.

This is our story, one of a Savior, a Sculptor, who lifts my chin so that I can look into his eyes and experience the greatest awakening of all.

TOUCH TOUCH

13

Touch

"Let's go and die with him."

That's what I told my friends, and at the time that's what I was willing to do.

At the time.

That was when Mary and Martha sent us word that their brother was sick. They asked Jesus to come but he declined, assuring us that Lazarus's illness wouldn't end in death.

Of course later, when he told us plainly that Lazarus was dead we were confused, especially when he suggested that he wanted to travel to Bethany, just outside of Jerusalem, and visit Mary and Martha.

Because just a few months earlier at the temple dedication there, the Jews had grabbed rocks to kill Jesus.

"But Lord," Peter said. "The Jews were trying to stone you there. You want to go back?"

And Jesus replied with a riddle about darkness and light, about how there are only twelve hours of light and a man doesn't stumble when he can see where he's going, but those who travel at night stumble because they can't see the path.

We had no idea what he was talking about.

Then Jesus told us that Lazarus was asleep and that he wanted to go to Bethany to wake him up.

Of course we thought that if he is sleeping he would awaken on his own and perhaps get better, but that's when Jesus told us that Lazarus was dead and that he was thankful we weren't there to see him earlier because now we would believe.

We were on the other side of the Jordan, more than a day's walk from Bethany, but I didn't care about that. I only cared about being close to the Lord. "Then," I said, "let's go. Let's all go. We'll die with you."

But no one died on that trip; instead Lazarus was brought back to life.

And when I saw what Jesus had done, what he could do, I did believe.

Seeing was believing.

Seeing.

Believing.

Yes, I'd offered to die with him in Jerusalem but then, not long afterward when I had the chance to, I ran off. We all did. Scattering into the night.

Gethsemane.

The soldiers and guards.

Torches and swords and confusion.

And then.

I ran.

He was taken away, and we were left to our shame and our shattered hopes. I was probably the most ashamed of all since I'd been the one to suggest we should all die by his side.

Dead.

Our Savior was dead.

There's nothing to do when your Savior dies except to pick up the pieces and move on, and that's what I was planning to do.

In the days following his death I slipped off by myself while the other disciples met together to plan their escape in case the Romans came for them too.

Then, Sunday night when I visited them in the dimly lit upper room, they told me they'd seen him, that he was alive. I just stared at them. "What are you talking about? He's dead. We all saw it. He—"

"No," Peter said, "I know that. I'm not talking about that, I'm talking about now."

"Now?"

"Yes, he was dead before, but now he's alive." I heard excitement in his voice, and also a note of frustration directed, no doubt, at me.

"No." I thought of all that I'd seen, all the miracles and signs, but also all the things Jesus couldn't do—when he failed to perform any impressive healings in his hometown where no one accepted that he was who he claimed to be. And telling us that he didn't know when the end of the world would come, or when he would return to the earth as he'd predicted.

When I thought of these things I was filled with a great sense of failure. I had failed him, yes, but he had also failed us. "No. He is dead."

"He told us about this," John said. "Remember? He said that it would happen: 'After three days the Son of Man will rise.' You remember that, don't you?"

Yes, I remembered his words, but none of us had believed them at the time and I didn't know why the others seemed to believe them now.

"Look," I said. "I'd need to see for myself."

Peter leapt to his feet. "Why can't you just believe us?"

"Would you believe you?"

A moment of silence crawled through the room.

I gestured toward Mary of Magdala, who was in the room with us, and asked Peter, "Did you believe Mary when she told you? Did you believe when you went to the tomb and found it empty?"

No reply.

"No, you didn't believe until you saw him for yourself, until he ate the fish with you—as you claim. So don't make it seem like I'm the only one here who—"

John gently set a hand on my arm. "No one is accusing you of anything, Thomas. We're just saying, this is what we know. We spoke with him. We touched him."

"When I speak with him," I said, "when I can touch him for myself, then I'll believe."

I wanted to believe them, truly I did, but I couldn't bring myself to do it. I needed more proof, but they had none to offer.

The next week seemed to last forever. With each day that passed, their smugness began to fade. We continued to pray, to meet, to talk, to hide from the constant eyes of the Romans, but Jesus didn't return.

By Wednesday they had stopped looking so confident.

By Thursday they started to tell me that just because I hadn't seen him didn't mean he wasn't alive.

"Then where is he? Why is he hiding?" I wasn't arguing. Honestly, I was just desperate to have some reason to believe, to have hope in my heart again. "If he really is alive and he's come back to initiate his kingdom, why hasn't he done it?"

And they had no answers.

Friday passed.

The Sabbath came and went. Still no sightings of the Lord.

Then Sunday arrived again. An entire week after their stories of seeing him alive, and if I'd had doubts earlier, I had them even more then.

We were together in the upper room when it happened.

By the looks on the faces of some of the men, I began to wonder if they were starting to doubt what they'd seen as well. Maybe he hadn't come back. Maybe they'd just dreamed the whole thing.

Maybe.

Maybe.

But then.

The stillness in the room gave birth to something else, a presence beside me.

It was as if the air parted, and stepping out of a crevice in time, he appeared.

Jesus.

Alive!

He greeted us with words of peace, but I was already on my knees. "My Lord and my God."

All of my doubts, my logic, bore in on me, a weight of failure and shame.

"Here, Thomas." He helped me to my feet. "Touch my hand." It was as if he'd read my thoughts, as if he knew exactly what kinds of doubts had curled up inside me.

He took my hand and brought it to his side and slid my fingers along the ridge of a deep and horrid wound.

His skin was warm to the touch, not cold like the skin of the dead.

As I removed my hand, my fingers were trembling.

Words escaped me.

"Lord," I begged. "Forgive me. Forgive me for doubting. Forgive me for—"

"You believe," he said. "There's nothing to forgive."

I glanced around the room, and rather than judgment on the faces of my friends, I saw only looks of shock. They'd seen him before, but they still looked as amazed as I was.

Overjoyed but also terrified.

"You've touched me, you've seen me, and now you believe. And your faith will be a blessing to you always." He paused, then added, "But those who haven't seen but only hear the story and believe, those who let faith lead them to sight, they will be blessed even more than you."

And then he embraced me and I knew for sure that this time, no matter what, I would die for him.

Die for the man who rose from the dead.

A week later his disciples were in the house again, and Thomas was with them. Though the doors were locked, Jesus came and stood among them and said, "Peace be with you!" Then he said to Thomas, "Put your finger here; see my hands. Reach out your hand and put it into my side. Stop doubting and believe." (John 20:26–27)

In 1904 H. G. Wells wrote a fictional short story entitled "The Country of the Blind," in which a mountaineer named Nunez falls unsuspectingly into an isolated village in the remote mountains of Ecuador. The villagers had long ago been cut off from the rest of civilization by an earthquake that shifted the neighboring mountains, sealing off the mountain passes that outsiders might have used to visit them.

Sometime later a disease had struck the villagers, causing all newborns to be born blind. For decades this went on, until the village had no collective memory of the visible world.

So, when Nunez stumbles upon the village, everyone is blind, and no one has any concept whatsoever of sight. At first, since he has the sense of sight that none of them possess, Nunez thinks he'll be able to enlighten and lead the people, but he soon finds that they dismiss him as mad since he talks about things they cannot even comprehend, such as "sky" or "clouds" or other villages. He could pretend, of course, that he can't see and that all of his talk about sight was just madness caused by his fall, but that would be a betrayal of the truth.

The villagers believe his eyeballs are the result of a disease that renders him mad. Then, eventually, when he falls in love with a young woman of the village, he agrees to their conditions for him to marry her—an operation that will remove his eyes.

However, early in the morning on the day of the scheduled operation, he scans the cliffs and sees a possible route out and decides to take his chances trying to climb the mountains and escape.

The story is full of interesting moral dilemmas—do you pretend to know less than others so that they will accept you? What's more important, love or freedom? Truth or acceptance?

But what strikes me most about the story is the idea that these people, born with only four senses, consider all of Nunez's talk of "sight" as madness and nonsense.

The first time I read the story I wondered how I would respond to someone who was trying to convince me that he had a sense that no one in my world had ever heard of, and that he tried to do his convincing by using words and descriptions that sounded meaningless.

I would have probably dismissed him as insane as well. Just as Jesus's own family members did with him (Mark 3:21).

The more I think about faith, the more I'm convinced that doubt is not the opposite of faith, but more like a crack in the side of it—a crack that might widen if enough wedges are driven into it. Rarely have I met someone who has faith without the fault lines of doubt running through it somewhere. And often, the people with blind, untested faith are the ones whose belief can be shattered with one giant hammer blow.

> I'm traversing the edge
> of this moment. Within it I
> find all that God has to offer;
> beyond it I find all that
> worry has to give.

The mists that cloud my vision can
only be called doubt,
the hands that grip the
rock can only be called
faith.

You'd never expect someone to see with his ears or hear with his skin or smell with his eyes. Each sense is designed to register the world in a different way. And if someone with a nose moved to a land where none of the people have the ability to smell, he might try to describe smells to them, but they wouldn't understand, would have no context to do so. "Prove to us that smells exist!" they'd say and he would reply, "How?"

And so, God doesn't speak to our ears or appear to our eyes or touch our skin, he's only sensed in the spirit, because he is Spirit. How could the spiritual ever be sensed by the physical? How can the incomprehensible be understood with the mind? I love how Annie Dillard describes this in *Traveling Mercies*. On her journey toward faith, she saw Jesus sitting in her room watching her with patience and love. She wrote, "I squinched my eyes shut, but that didn't help because that's not what I was seeing him with."

And so those who have turned off the spiritual frequencies in their souls say, "Prove that God exists!" and we say, "How?" for the very means with which we would prove him to them relies on the spiritual senses they aren't willing to use.

A man said to Plato, "You are the one who says there is a world other than this one, and a human being other than this one."
Plato said, "Yes."

The man said, "Then show me."

Plato said, "You don't have what it takes to see it."[6]

I don't have any idea how we could describe the color purple to a man who has never been able to see. How can you describe the heart of God to someone who has never learned to believe? The best we can hope for is to give hints and whispers of the inexplicable, of the invisible God who speaks in the language of the soul, whispering to us beneath the skin of the visible.

One of the deep enigmas of God is this: he is always available, yet not visible. He has filled the world with hints of his presence, but not overwhelming proof of his existence. The blessing comes when we believe not when we demand proof.

The temptation to doubt will always be there. But learning to live by faith rather than sight is one of the keys to the Christian life. As the eighteenth-century priest Jean-Pierre de Caussade wrote, "If we want to live a life of faith we must fight without pause against our senses."[7]

Jesus's invitation and promises are wrapped around himself and not just his words, around his presence, not just his principles. We learn faith by coming to him and we overcome fear and worry by letting him have our doubts as well as our agendas; by coming to him for peace, not just listening to his teachings for guidance.

Because as Thomas learned that night when he touched the Savior's wounds and heard the Savior's words, seeing isn't always believing, but the essence of believing is seeing when there's nothing there to see.

And that's where the richest blessings are found.

CAUGHT IN THE THORNS
CAUGHT IN THE THORNS
CAUGHT IN THE THORNS
CAUGHT IN THE THORNS
CAUGHT IN THE THORNS
CAUGHT IN THE THORNS
CAUGHT IN THE THORNS
CAUGHT IN THE THORNS
CAUGHT IN THE THORNS
CAUGHT IN THE THORNS
CAUGHT IN THE THORNS
CAUGHT IN THE THORNS
CAUGHT IN THE THORNS
CAUGHT IN THE THORNS

14

Caught in the Thorns

Rome

Dusk

AD 66

I watched him for a long time, sleeping on the stone floor, chained up like a dog. I'd already made my decision. Last night. I was only here today to say good-bye. But I wasn't sure how to say it.

Finally, as the dim light slanted through the prison bars, he began to stir.

"Paul?" I said. "Are you awake?"

He opened his eyes slowly. "Demas?"

"Yes."

He blinked his eyes to orient himself. "Good of you to come."

"Yes."

His arms and legs were chained to the wall. He sat up as best he could. "Praise God for the grace of Jesus."

"Yes," I said.

He did not look well. His age was showing, and in recent years his health problems had only gotten worse, especially since his latest arrest and imprisonment in this cell. Damp. Musky. Smelling of urine and mildew and death.

And now, with winter on the way, I knew his condition would only worsen. But soon none of that would matter much. He was to be executed for being a follower of the Way. The date had been set.

"I'm here to say good-bye," I said.

I thought I heard him whisper something, but I couldn't be sure. It might have just been echoes. He stared past me at the blank wall behind me.

When he didn't reply, I said, "I can't stay any longer. This isn't what I . . ." The words didn't come easily so I just let my voice trail off.

I knew what people would say. Of course I knew. But I'd finally come to the point in my life where I didn't care. It was time for me to move on.

Still he didn't respond.

"Good-bye, Paul."

Silence.

"I said, good-bye."

"I heard you."

I held back a sigh. I didn't want it to end like this. We'd been friends for over eight years, ever since he first arrived in Rome. "It doesn't have to be like this," I said.

Stale water dripped somewhere out of sight. That was all.

"Please," I said. "We've been through so much together. Talk to me. You weren't angry at Titus or Crescens when they left."

Finally, he looked at me. "Why are you doing this, my friend?" He coughed a harsh and gasping cough and leaned back against the wall of his cell. "Please. Tell me that much."

I didn't really know what to say. Putting the reasons into words was difficult. Life is short. I had plans. Things I wanted to do. A life I'd put on hold. But it wasn't that simple.

"Because," I said finally, "I don't want to end up like you."

I didn't mean for the words to have barbs on them, but by the look on his face I knew they had hurt him. Thinking back, I know I shouldn't have said that, even though it summed up everything I'd been feeling.

Paul nodded. "Yes. Good-bye then, Demas."

So I turned to leave. And as I walked toward the door at the end of the narrow hallway I heard soft noises coming from his cell. It sounded like crying.

One of Paul's closest friends was a man named Barnabas. I first met him a few years ago, and we hit it off right away.

Barnabas was an easygoing sort of guy while Paul could be a bit harsh and argumentative. Judgmental even. Barnabas always had a kind word, so it didn't surprise me when he told me about the early days of the church and how close-knit everyone was. Of course, he didn't draw attention to it, but I already knew he was a big part of that. People were selling their land and pooling the money together to share with everyone else. (Barnabas had been the first one to do it. Luke told me about that later on.)

"No one had any needs," Barnabas told me one day. "We provided for each other. It was the way it should be, Demas, the way things were meant to be. Until . . ." His voice trailed off.

"Until what?"

"Until Ananias and Sapphira sold their land." His voice had taken a softer turn.

"So what happened? What changed?"

Barnabas looked sadder than I'd ever seen him. "No one knew it at the time, but when they brought their money, they kept back some of it for themselves."

I wasn't quite sure I understood. "They were greedy?"

Barnabas shook his head. "The money wasn't the issue. They lied about it to Peter. They lied about it to God. They said they'd brought the whole amount." He became intense, leaning forward, a fire burning in his eyes. "And right in front of everyone, they fell over dead. Everyone was afraid then, Demas. Afraid of God. Afraid of us."

I watched him for a moment. His face, tense and drawn, and I felt a deep awkwardness growing between us. "But why would God do that? Kill off two of his followers?"

A long moment passed. Finally, he said, "With God, there are no secrets, Demas. The one thing he can't stand is people pretending to be more spiritual than they really are." Then he looked at me deeply, tenderly. "Praise God for the grace of Jesus."

"Praise God for the grace of Jesus," I said.

I never actually met Jesus face-to-face. I mean, I did meet him in a sense, but I never had the chance to actually talk to him like Paul did on the road to Damascus. Maybe if I had, things would have turned out differently. I don't know.

Paul was the one who first introduced me to Jesus, through his letter to the people here in Rome. So later, when Paul arrived here, I stayed with him. Through it all. Through the house arrests, the trials, the reprieves, the latest imprisonment. I had to give up a lot of my dreams to do it too. And for a long time I thought it was worth it.

Luke and I would sit with Paul for hours: Luke bent over his parchments, Paul laying there in chains, talking about how much he loved to suffer for Jesus. How it made him feel closer to the Lord Jesus Christ and how we should all feel closer to Jesus by suffering too. Personally, I could think of other ways to feel close to someone.

Of course, I didn't say anything at the time. I just listened, or tried to. Sometimes my mind wandered.

In those days, Luke was working on a book about the life of Jesus. Sometimes he'd tell me the stories he was writing down, the ones Jesus used to tell.

Luke's favorite was about a farmer. I heard him tell it so often, I can just about recite it from memory.

So, there was this farmer, right? And he planted seeds by scattering them in his field. Some fell on the hard, trampled path and were eaten by birds. Some fell on the shallow, rocky soil where they grew quickly, but then withered in the sun because they didn't get enough water. Others fell among the thorns, where they took root but were slowly choked out. And a few of the seeds fell on the good soil and produced a bumper crop.

That's the whole story. But everything in it has a hidden meaning. That's the way these things work. The seed is the Word of God. The soil on the path represents the people who don't understand the word and the devil snatches it from their hearts. The rocky soil is those who accept the message with joy, but in the time of testing and persecution they fall away. I've met those kind of people. Ministered beside them. I've watched them wither. It isn't pretty.

At this point in the story, Luke would lean forward—you should hear me tell it, I can sound just like him. "The soil with the thorns are those who hear the Word but get choked by life's riches, worries, and pleasures."

And, of course, the good soil represents those who have a good and noble heart, persevere, and produce a crop. There you go. The parable of the farmer and the seeds.

I don't know exactly when I started questioning my decision to become a follower of the Way. Maybe last year. Maybe the year before. It's hard to pinpoint.

I've seen friends of mine get beaten, tortured, imprisoned. I've seen women get fed to the lions and men get skinned alive. And for what? Because they refused to stop telling people about the Way? All for a story?

To what end? How does getting beaten to death, or hunted down like a wild animal, or slaughtered for entertainment benefit God or anyone else? And there's so much we've had to give up. I mean, when I started out as a follower of the Way, I had no idea the path would lead me here—to a prison cell listening to an old man talk about the joy of pain.

Luke told me that Jesus talked all the time about denying yourself, taking up a cross, losing your life, selling everything you owned, giving up everything, and following him.

Well, I guess I was tired of giving up everything. It was time to get some of my life back.

The last time Luke told me the seed story, he hesitated at the end and then said, "Demas, sometimes I worry about you."

"What are you talking about?"

He looked at me intensely, with those sharp incisive eyes. "Don't get caught in the thorns, Demas."

"What?"

"The thorns. Don't get caught."

"I won't."

He was silent.

"Really, I won't. Why are you saying that? Don't worry. I won't."

"Okay."

"Praise God for the grace of Jesus," I said.

"Praise God for the grace of Jesus," he replied.

In the end, I wished I could have told Luke myself, but he wasn't there that day and I didn't really want to track him down just to hear him say "I told you so." He'll find out soon enough, I guess. Paul will tell him. Who knows. Maybe I'll run into him on the street or something. I doubt it, though. I think I'll travel for a while. Do some sightseeing.

I wonder if I'll show up in that letter Paul is writing to Timothy. If I do, I can only imagine what kind of things Paul will say about me. Oh well. That's all in the past now.

I press open the door and walk away from Paul and the Way. There are other paths to follow now, other voices to listen to. I hear them calling me forward. Sweet voices. Promises of a new beginning.

Call them thorns if you want to. I call them my future.

[Timothy] please come as soon as you can. Demas has deserted me because he loves the things of this life and has gone to Thessalonica. Crescens has gone to Galatia, and Titus has gone to Dalmatia. Only Luke is with me.

—Paul, in his second letter to Timothy (2 Tim. 4:9–11 NLT)

The story of Demas hits a little too close to home.

His name only appears a few times in the Bible. In Philemon 1:24 and Colossians 4:14 Paul mentions that Demas sent greetings to the believers in those churches. Apparently Demas was one of the leaders of the early church and a close friend and associate of Paul. He must have been well-known and highly respected among the community of believers or Paul wouldn't have mentioned him in his letters.

But the last time Demas's name appears, in 2 Timothy 4, we see him deserting Paul because, as Paul put it, "he loves the things of this life." After that, Demas disappeared into history. We never hear of him again. Demas loved the things of this life. That's his legacy.

And all too often it is also mine.

Because I hear the thorns call to me as well.

Riches, worries, and pleasure—the hallmarks of our culture, the thorns snagging the children of God.

The things of this world aren't all bad, of course. There's nothing wrong with loving a glorious sunset, or a sky full of stars, or the smell of a mountain meadow, or the laughter of a child, or a bite of a perfectly seasoned chicken fajita. I know God created those things and called them "good." (At least the first four. I'm pretty sure he would've called the chicken fajita good too. But Scripture doesn't specifically mention it.)

Of course it's not wrong to love the things that God loves. The problem comes when we become entangled in greed, pride, or lust: "For the world offers only the lust for physical pleasure, the lust for everything we see, and pride in our possessions. These are not from the Father. They are from this evil world" (1 John 2:16 NLT).

So there you go. Thorns by another name.

If there's one thing Jesus made clear in his teaching it's this: following him is costly. It always requires sacrifice. Finally, after twenty-two years of being a Christian I'm beginning to learn the troubling, liberating, shocking lesson that if my Christianity costs me nothing, it's not Christianity. If I'm living a comfortable, easy, reasonable life pursuing riches, popularity, and a good reputation, I'm following something other than Jesus.

This world is all too willing to offer us thorns disguised as success, a good reputation, and financial security.

Demas's story is a painful one to retell because I've seen people I care about, people I love, get caught in the thorns. It's heart-wrenching. Even as the thorns are choking their spiritual lives, the people keep unwittingly wrapping the nettles tighter and tighter around their necks by their choices, lifestyles, priorities, investments. And I've seen the results. You have too: short tempers, road rage, abortions, addictions, ruined reputations, shattered marriages, compromised commitments, lack of compassion, shortsightedness. All that junk of modern life. Fallout from the thorns.

And it's not just other people. It's me too. The minute I get caught up gazing at the seductive brambles of popularity or the good life, the thorns take root again and grow thicker and deeper in the materialistic soil of my heart. So, my story ends up mirroring Demas's.

He loved the things of this life. And so do I.

For the past few years I've been praying the words of David in Psalm 86:11–12: "Teach me your way, O LORD, and I will walk in your truth; give me an undivided heart, that I may fear your name. I will praise you, O Lord my God, with all my heart." Since David had to pray for an undivided heart, I'm guessing we can infer that his heart was divided at the time he penned those words. Anyone familiar with his story can see the thorns that grew there—thorns of lust, fear, pleasure, murder, and pride. Even though he was a man of God ("a man after God's own heart" [Acts 13:22]), his heart became divided by the same thorns that infest my heart today.

I think the story of the seeds and the sower describes not just the four ways people respond to the gospel but the four ways each of us tend to respond to it at different points in our lives. Sometimes my heart is rocky and I don't want to hear the Word. I don't understand it; I resist it. Sometimes the soil of my soul is shallow—my joy withers away during times of trouble and heartache and rejection and my convictions become scorched by my circumstances.

And yes, occasionally God's Word sprouts up and he shows me fruit that he was able to grow through my life, though I can hardly understand how. However the parable touches me most personally when Jesus talks about the thorns. All too often I feel like I'm standing at the perimeter of a great hedge, hacking away at the thorns that just don't want to stay down.

Once when the thorns had grown too high in my life, I wrote this prayer. I find that I have to pray it in some way almost every day.

Untangle me, Jesus.
Uproot the thorns in my life.
Cultivate the soil of my heart.
I'm so quickly ensnared,
so easily entangled in
    the worries and riches and pleasures of life,
    and the many alluring brambles of this world.
Give me an undivided heart;
that I might fear your name,
    walk in your truth,
    and produce a crop that lasts.

I used to think God would answer this prayer all at once, that all my struggles would disappear and I'd be able to run through fields of daisies like that nun in *The Sound of Music*, rather than pick my way through the misty forest among all the lurking nettles like usual. But instead, I've found that this is one prayer God prefers to answer little by little by snipping away one thorny branch at a time, often as it's reaching out for me from the shadows.

Sometimes I'm tempted to throw in the towel like Demas did, to abandon my faith and give in to the struggle; just close my eyes and leap headfirst into the brambles. And, left on my own, I probably would. I almost have. But something keeps holding me back. "Help me, Jesus," I whisper. "Lead me in your ways. Give me an undivided heart." And something arrives just in the nick of time to keep the thorns far enough at bay once again. I think I know its name.

It's called grace.

15

Leaving the Boat

I look across the water toward the open sea and watch the waves drain sunlight from the day.

And I think of my children.

Scattered throughout the land.

Not children by a father's will but children born of the promise. Of course, they're not mine really, they're his. But I had the honor of sharing the story with them, of seeing the light of understanding come to their eyes, of being present the moment new life was born.

So many of them hurting so much.

Power-hungry, yes. Some are. Living in wounded relationships, under the curse of broken promises and splintered dreams. Some in danger of losing their lives. Some already have.

I close my eyes and take in a breath of the salty air.

A few gulls cry out in the distance.

Even after all these years, it feels strange to be here on a shoreline without a fishing boat. Exiled in a place that reminds me so much of home, and yet feels so far away. The strain of familiarity tugging at my isolation.

My brother and my father and I used to spend so many nights on the sea, talking in the cool moonlight. It was a common enough life, and it felt natural, like the way things should be.

Well, it almost did.

I remember one tired morning in particular when we were fixing our nets—that was the day everything changed.

The waves caught the early morning sunlight and tossed it back to us. Playful. As if it were alive itself.

Nearby I saw the rabbi walking along the shore toward us. A couple of my friends were with him—Peter and Andrew. I recognized the teacher right away. We'd heard of him. His name was Jesus.

As he approached I glanced at my brother who was just looking up from his work, and my father who was staring silently at the rabbi.

And then Jesus called to me. To all of us. "Come on!" His voice was strong and clear, just like the day. "Follow me."

I'll always remember that look on my father's face. The look of disapproval.

"Come on," Jesus called again. "And I'll make you fishers of men."

"Fishers of men?" James mumbled. "What's a fisher of men?"

The words were a mystery to me too, but a mystery that reverberated through me, called me to an adventure, invited me into a mystery.

"Come on," I said to my father and James. "Let's go."

"We can't just . . ." my father began.

I leapt onto the beach, and a moment later James joined me.

My father stayed in the boat.

Of course, he wasn't the age to become a follower of a young rabbi. And he had a business to run. And he couldn't just pick up everything and leave to follow a man like this.

Those were the reasons he told me later. But whatever he was thinking that day, he didn't follow. He stayed in the boat.

It always struck me that he stayed in the boat.

Later, despite all that James and I said to him over the years, despite all that has happened since we became fishers of men, followers of the rabbi, my father never left his nets.

It is one of the greatest pains of my life.

He died before he stepped out of the boat.

The sea stretches before me and I think of my children.

And my father.

And the sky grows darker.

The Romans have banished me to this island, Patmos. A prison not just for my body, but also for my spirit, since they were separating me from my new family, brothers and sisters of the Son, children of faith.

I've written to them over the years, to these new converts, told them that God is love and he has sacrificed for all of us. Explained that in order to show our love for him we must put his commands into practice and love others, not just with words or with tongue, but with actions and with truth.

And sometimes they listen.

And sometimes they don't.

So many memories of the time I spent with the Lord.

The long nights around those campfires, listening to Peter crack jokes and Jesus tell stories. The days at the temple when he spoke in a way that brought everything together, that actually made the law and the teachings of the prophets I'd heard as a child make sense.

And then there were the miracles: turning the water into wine, healings, casting out demons, calming storms. And that day on the mountain when he was transfigured into a heavenly being of light. And of course the day he rose from the dead.

But what strikes me now are the riddles—the first will be last, the last first; if you want to lead you must be a servant. And the names he gave himself: the Good Shepherd. The Way. The Truth. He told us that living water would come to all who follow him.

Water that would never leave us thirsty again.

But still I do thirst. Somehow he both quenches my thirst for all that is real and instills in me a thirst for more truth, more love than I ever dreamed was possible.

He's coming back. That will be my next letter—a collection of the visions, the revelations, he has given me.

And what shall I say?

Only what I've been told: don't worry, don't give up, don't be afraid. Prepare, persevere, share the story. And be ready, because he is coming soon.

I sit on the shore, take up my pen and my scroll, and I pray that these words will be a comfort to my children.

And I write.

I saw the holy city, the new Jerusalem, coming down from God out of heaven like a beautiful bride prepared for her husband.

I heard a loud shout from the throne, saying, "Look, the home of God is now among his people! He will live with them, and they will be his people. God himself will be with them. He will remove all of their sorrows, and there will be no more death or sorrow or crying or pain. For the old world and its evils are gone forever."

—A description of the new life to come (Rev. 21:2–4)

One day after speaking at a youth camp in Michigan I got an entirely new look at God's grace. I was sitting at a table with a couple of teenage girls and one of them told me she'd had two pets in her life.

"What happened to them?" I asked.

"They both died."

"How?"

"Well, the bunny died when I was doing bunny rides. And the goldfish I squished. I never got another pet."

"Bunny rides?"

"Yup. I was four at the time. He seemed about the right size."

Then the girl on the other side of me cut in, "I had a gerbil and I didn't know you weren't supposed to give them a bath. So I took him in the bathroom and I put water into the sink and put him in, and then I took toilet paper and I was wiping him off and I flushed the toilet and he jumped out of my hands into the toilet. And I reached in and saved him."

The bunny-riding girl's eyes lit up. "That's what God did! We jumped out of God's hands into the toilet of sin. But he reached down into the world and rescued us!"

There's nothing like lessons on grace from a drowning gerbil.

Grace and obedience form a paradoxical facet of the Christian life.

God calls us to obey, but when we fail he offers us grace. Yet that doesn't excuse sin or cheapen the sacrifice it takes for him to forgive us.

In other words: yes, God rescues us when we jump into the toilet of sin, but that doesn't mean we should keep doing it. After all, why would we want to?

Here's a good question to ask about our choices: does this choice promote or undermine the story God is trying to tell the world?

Choosing the way of the kingdom was central to the message of Jesus. So as we shape the choices we make, it's wise to ask: is my life promoting his kingdom—the one built on the rock (his teachings and person)—or promoting the kingdom of this world—the one built on sand (my "natural" tendencies to look out for myself and choose the way that always promotes me)?

Following Jesus, living the life of a believer, is about a change of attitude, action, belief, imagination, agenda, priority, pursuit, affection, understanding, relationship, emotion—it's the reorientation of all aspects of being human. "You are weak in your natural selves. Just as you used to offer the parts of your body in slavery to impurity and to ever-increasing wickedness, so now offer them in slavery to righteousness leading to holiness" (Rom. 6:19).

God doesn't want my promises or good intentions, he wants my will. Obedience isn't something we can plan to do. It's something we either do or don't do. Jesus never said, "Promise me you'll follow me," "Promise me you'll believe in me," "Promise me you'll forsake your life and deny yourself." Instead he simply says, "Follow. Believe. Forsake. Deny."

> But those who obey God's word really do love him. That is the way to know whether or not we live in him. (1 John 2:5)

Although we can (at least outwardly) obey God without loving him, we cannot love God apart from obeying him. To put it bluntly, the only way to show love for God is by obeying him. Lack of obedience toward God is evidence of a lack of love for God. We cannot express our love for him by disobeying him. It's simply not possible.

But we will fail.

Of course we will.

It's not hypocrisy to have high ideals and aspirations but fail to live up to them. It's called being human.

We have to step out of the boat, and when we slip, accept his hand to lift us to our feet once again. It's his specialty.

In Galatians, Paul mentions that self-control is a "fruit of the Spirit." I find that fascinating.

Since it's called *self*-control, I would have thought it would come from the *self*, but Paul doesn't say that. Instead he explains that self-control is a fruit of a healthy relationship with God's Spirit. Self-control isn't the fruit of effort or conviction or hard work or self-discipline. It's the fruit that God's Spirit naturally grows in our lives when we don't constantly nip it in the bud.

When we walk step by step, moment by moment with him.

Remember that when Jesus was talking about removing from our lives the things that cause us to sin, he didn't say, "If your right hand causes you to sin, say three Hail Marys," or "sit under a tree and meditate for a while," or "go join a men's accountability group, fast, read two chapters of the Bible, and then tell yourself you're special inside."

He didn't give a spiritual answer to the problem; he gave a physical one—cut that stuff out of your life.

We can each take specific steps to decrease the influence and power that temptation has over our lives.

And we can do this in practical ways, especially when we remember that the source of most of the temptations that dog us isn't the world around us but the world within us.

Evil desires don't come simply from our surroundings but from deep within our own hearts. No matter where we go—a monastery in Tibet, a cathedral in Rome, a temple in Jerusalem, or up in the hills of eastern Tennessee, we will always be faced with temptation. Jesus put it this way, "It is the thought-life that defiles you. For from within, out of a person's heart, come evil thoughts, sexual immorality, theft, murder, adultery, greed, wickedness, deceit, eagerness for lustful pleasure, envy, slander, pride, and foolishness" (Mark 7:20–22).

You and I can't get away from the problem of rebellion because everywhere we go we take the problem with us. Splintered hearts in a splintered world. Our world isn't the way it should be because we're not the way we should be.

And yet, in the stunning paradox of grace, though the world might overwhelm us, we have already overcome it.

Everyone born of God overcomes the world. This is the victory that has overcome the world, even our faith. Who is it that overcomes the world? Only he who believes that Jesus is the Son of God. (1 John 5:4–5)

His love overcomes our failings, our past, our doubts, the times we fall into temptation. This victory is his, and when faith lives in our hearts, the final victory and an eternity of celebration is ours as well.

Thanks
and
Acknowledgments

Special thanks to Pam Johnson, Tom Vick, and Kristin Kornoelje for their editorial work and research assistance. You made the job that much easier and the book that much better.

Notes

1. A caveat—the stories in this book are based on actual characters, instances, and events in the Bible, but I took some creative license, trying to climb into the characters' thoughts and inner world. In no way is this meant to show disregard or disrespect for the Scriptures. Rather, I'm hoping to tell you some familiar stories in new ways so that you'll walk away with a greater respect for Scripture and a deeper connection with God.

2. Taken from Psalm 51.

3. Peter Kreeft, ed., *Christianity for Modern Pagans: Pascal's Pensees* (San Francisco: Ignatius Press, 1993), 168.

4. Robert Bly, James Hillman, and Michael Meade, eds., *The Rag and Bone Shop of the Heart* (New York: Harper Perennial, 1993), 417–18.

5. C. S. Lewis, *The Pilgrim's Regress*, 1933.

6. Taken from *Living a Good Life: Advice on Virtue, Love, and Action from the Ancient Greek Masters*, trans. Thomas Cleary (Boston, London: Shambhala Publications, 1997), 46.

7. Jean-Pierre de Caussade, *Abandonment to the Divine Providence*.

Steven James is a bestselling author and award-winning storyteller. He has written many collections of short fiction, scripts, novels, and inspirational books that explore the paradox of good and evil in our world. He lives at the base of the Blue Ridge Mountains with his wife and three daughters.

Come Meet

STEVEN JAMES at

www.stevenjames.net

Learn fun facts about the Patrick Bowers Thrillers, sign up to receive updates, and more.

What if you **talked to GOD** like you talk to your friends?

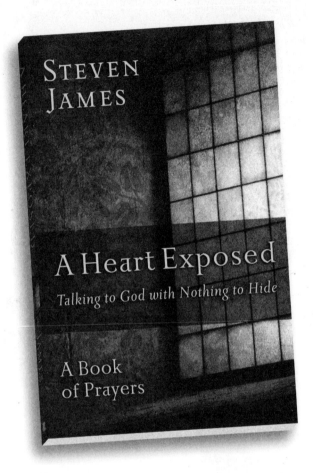

STEVEN JAMES

A Heart Exposed

Talking to God with Nothing to Hide

A Book of Prayers

Critically acclaimed and bestselling author

STEVEN JAMES

will inspire you to a more powerful and honest prayer life.

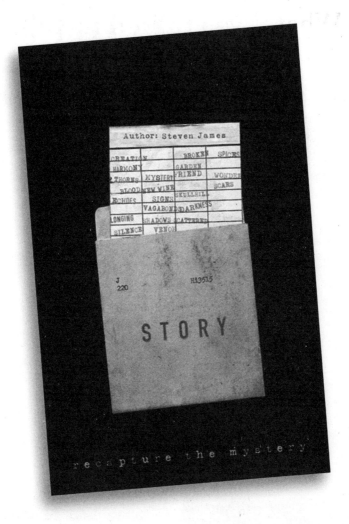

"A journey full of wonder, tears, joy, despair, and hope revealed through the eyes and heart of a storyteller."

—*Publishers Weekly*, starred review

STEVEN JAMES'S
critically acclaimed, spine-tingling,

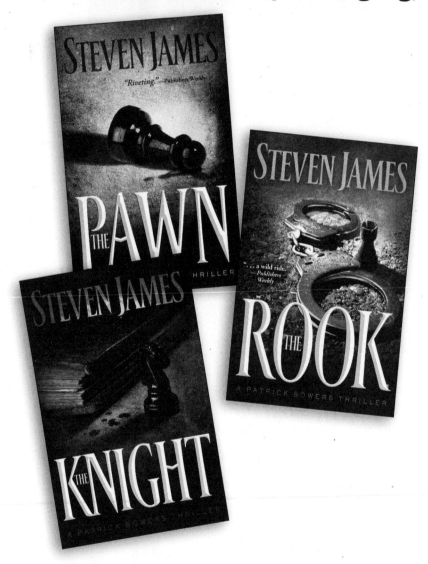

heart-stopping suspense series
THE BOWERS FILES